ISBN EBOOK: 978-1-64873-230-0
ISBN Paperback: 978-1-64873-232-4
ISBN Hardcover: 978-1-64873-231-7

Printed in the United States of America
Published by: Writer's Publishing House
Prescott, Az 86301

Cover and Interior Design Creative Artistic Excellence

Project Management and Book Launch by Writers Publishing House

Reclaim Your Reach

Alternative Media
Business/Marketing Guide

By Lizzy McNett

Acknowledgment

TruthSocial.com

On Oct. 27, 2022 Trump announced the launch date to a new social media platform called "TRUTH Social," which he said would help Americans "stand up to the tyranny of Big Tech."

The decision was announced just nine months ago. Twitter, Facebook, and Instagram banned U.S. President Donald Trump from social media.

According to Fox News, "the final launch will take place in the first quarter of 2022. TRUTH Social is part of Trump's new company, Trump Media & Technology Group (TMTG)."

He stated, "I created TRUTH Social and TMTG to stand up to the tyranny of Big Tech. We live in a world where the Taliban has a huge presence on Twitter, yet your favorite American President has been silenced. This is unacceptable."

"I am excited to send my first TRUTH on TRUTH Social very soon," Trump continued. "TMTG was founded with a mission to give a voice to all. I'm excited to soon begin sharing my thoughts on TRUTH Social and to fight back against Big Tech. Everyone asks me why doesn't someone stand up to Big Tech? Well, we will be soon!"

Trump is not the only person Big Tech has censored since the Jan. 6 Capitol Hill riots.

Read Also: Twitter Permanently Suspends Project Veritas, James O'Keefe

TRUTH Social is not the only action the former President has taken against Big Tech in the name of freedom of speech.

In early July, Trump filed lawsuits against industry leaders like Mark Zuckerberg and Jack Dorsey.

Movieguide® previously reported:

Former U.S. President Donald Trump announced he is suing Big Tech CEOs including Facebook's Mark Zuckerberg, Twitter's Jack Dorsey, and Google's Sundar Pichai over alleged censorship.

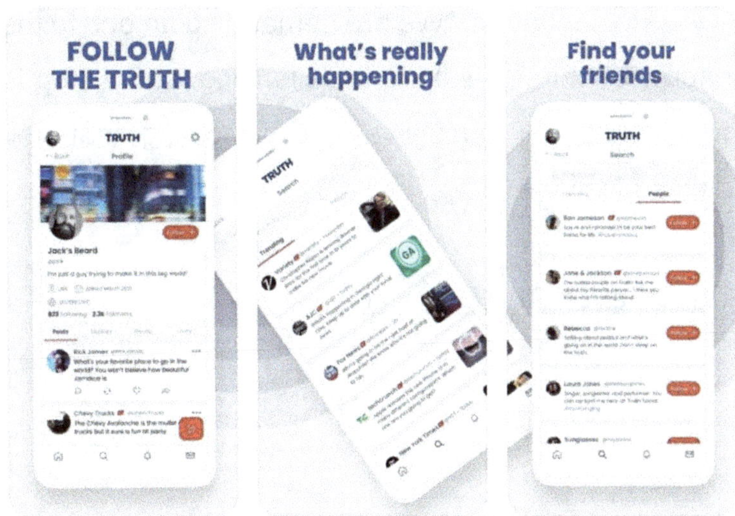

"I'm filing as the lead class representative a major class-action lawsuit against the big tech giants, including Facebook, Google, and Twitter, as well as their executives," Trump said. "We're going to hold big tech accountable."

Trump called the lawsuit "a very beautiful development for our freedom of speech."

He continued: "We are demanding an end to the shadow-banning, a stop to the silencing, and a stop to the blacklisting, banishing, and canceling that you know so well."

Subscribe for TruthSocial.com

What is Free Speech?

First Amendment

Congress shall make no law respecting an establishment of religion, or prohibiting the free exercise thereof; or abridging the freedom of speech, or of the press, or the right of the people peaceably to assemble, and to petition the Government for a redress of grievances.

According to Brandon Gaille of Small Business & Marketing Advice, "1.72 billion people is the number of people that are affected by internet censorship on any given day."

In America, the Constitution gives every citizen the right to Free Speech according to the First Amendment. The law grants the right to express your thoughts freely. It includes freedom of expression either in writing or orally to the people. Free speech is a constitutionally defended human right, one that is bestowed upon everyone regardless of gender, sex, religion, race, nationality, or any other identifying factor.

The amendment provides a baseline for our unshakeable right to support any beliefs. We the people were given the right not to be censored for speaking out against any issues, especially if they pertain to the government or its actors. Under no circumstances should anyone be silenced for professing their beliefs; as long as they are not breaking any laws.

Freedom of speech encourages people to actively look for dissenting arguments, and challenge the popular narrative. Freethinkers are the foundations of society. They produce the philosophical thought necessary to drive morals and ethics in the right direction. Free speech encourages a cultural drive to maximize everyone's lifestyle.

Any worthwhile society must function without the interference of government, by avoiding the censorship of free speech. It then provides honest open communication, provoking transparency.

We the people must never stop fighting for our right to free speech. The loss of our God-given rights will be the failure of America.

Table of Contents

Chapter One:

What is marketing?

By definition, marketing is "the process or technique of promoting, selling, and distributing a product or service." But the art of marketing is far more than just assembling product lines or writing simplified phrases. It takes time and dedication to create a unique campaign for each individual company or business.

Writer's Publishing House has developed an exceptional process. A strong marketing strategy grows out of a company's value proposition, allowing the client's campaigns to shine above the competition.

The best marketing campaigns revolve around product solicitation. For example, Walmart markets itself as a discount retailer with "everyday low prices." A company does not create a marketing strategy from scratch. Instead, it starts with the value proposition and distills the campaign from those core messages.

The foundation of effective marketing is matching the customer's needs to the right products or services.

Proper marketing eliminates the struggle to find your potential customer. When a business owner creates content designed to address the consumer's needs, it attracts qualified prospects and builds trust based on shared interests.

A good marketing campaign educates the potential customer. People do not want to be sold to. The best approach is to communicate through your knowledge and expertise in the field you practice. When someone clearly understands a concept, it becomes easy for them to make an informed decision.

In the Writer's Publishing House Marketing Resource Guide, readers will find a step-by-step process to develop exceptional marketing campaigns—campaigns that can compete with large companies that have fully staffed departments dedicated to product marketing. Once you learn the key fundamentals of social media networking and website basics, creating professional campaigns becomes much simpler.

Understanding the Importance of Marketing

What Does Marketing Mean?

The term "marketing" includes many activities, all connected to selling your company's products and services. Advertising is the most visible part, but consumer research is equally important. At its core, marketing is about matching the customer's needs to the right product or service. Proper marketing removes the struggle of finding your potential customer. When a business owner creates content that addresses consumer needs, it attracts qualified prospects and builds trust based on compatible interests.

Never confuse marketing with sales. While the two work together, they serve very different functions. Strong marketing platforms enable sales by transforming potential customers into long-term clients.

The marketing team must work closely to build a strong advertising campaign based on value at every stage of the customer's journey. The process of attracting, engaging, and delighting consumers builds trust and helps your company grow.

Some key marketing strategies include these actions:

Determine the type of product needed through consumer research and by studying sales patterns of similar goods or services.

- Modify existing products or services to align with current market patterns.
- Analyze the best ways to reach potential clients and make them aware of the products and services you offer.
- Design marketing campaigns based on the data you compiled.
- Confirm customer relationships using follow-up campaigns or loyalty programs.

A good marketing campaign educates the potential customer. People do not want to be sold. The best option is to communicate through your knowledge and expertise. When a person understands a concept clearly, it is easy for them to make an informed decision.

I Don't Know What to Say on Social Media

Social media marketing is one of the most cost-effective targeting tools available, but only when a business follows simple, proven guidelines. Not all platforms are a good fit for every business, which is why consumer research is so important. Once you choose the right platforms, the next step is learning what to post and how to avoid common pitfalls.

You might be wondering, "What do I say? Or how do I write a good post?" Let's discuss that for a moment.

Here are the recommendations from Writer's Publishing House:

Pinpoint an objective. Begin with clear goals, then determine how you will achieve them.

Create your authority. Every business owner or manager must establish themselves as an authority in their field. Why should someone do business with you? What do you have to offer?

Write posts to gain interaction. The best way to earn free advertising on most platforms is through likes, comments, and shares. As engagement grows, so does the visibility of your posts.

Show appreciation. Social media is not a monologue for bragging. That turns followers off. Interact in a genuine way. People can tell when a post is authentic. Like, share, and respond to others.

Stand out from the rest. Build a personal brand that conveys a clear persona the public will recognize.

Set a goal. This work requires both time and money. Know exactly what you want to convey, then track the results.

Lead with one platform. Use consumer data to target your ideal customer. Claim your profiles, but focus on mastering one platform at a time. Start by sharing relevant content, then gradually develop your own campaigns.

Create a social media calendar. Planning your posts creates consistency, which leads to better results.

Use visual content. Most users have short attention spans. Lengthy posts often go unnoticed. Use high-quality photos and short videos instead.

Get help when needed. Small business owners are short on time, and inconsistency hurts results. Writer's

Publishing House can be a valuable partner in reaching your social media marketing goals.

Social media marketing can feel impossible to master, especially when you are already handling every aspect of running a small business. But you are not alone. With the right guidance, anyone can succeed on social media. Recent data shows that social media remains one of the highest-ROI channels for small businesses, with many marketers planning to increase their investment in 2026.

Chapter Two:

The Importance of Marketing Strategies

Breaking Down Marketing Strategy

Marketing strategies are often confused with marketing plans. Because they do feed off one another, it is not unusual to find the marketing strategy and the marketing plan baked together into a single document. Although the transition between the two is blurry, a marketing strategy covers the big picture of what the business offers: the value proposition and related brand messaging. The marketing plan is how the business will get across the key message: the platforms, the creative, the timing, and so on. The marketing strategy may also be absorbed upwards into corporate value statements and other strategy documents.

The Creation of a Marketing Strategy

A marketing strategy grows out of a company's value proposition. The value proposition summarizes the competitive advantage a company has in its market. The value proposition usually provides a key message for all marketing. Walmart, for example, is a discount retailer with "everyday low prices," and its business operations and marketing revolve around that. A company is never creating a marketing strategy from scratch; they start with the value proposition and distill the key marketing message(s) from that.

Once the value proposition is succinctly stated, the hard work is done. Any marketing asset, from a print ad design to a social media campaign, can be judged by how well it communicates the value proposition. To further the efficiency of marketing efforts, market research can be added to the marketing strategy to identify untapped audiences or refine the target consumer. Finally, an overall goal for the marketing strategy can be set, with all the subsequent marketing plans inheriting the responsibility for delivering on it. These can be concrete, bottom-line goals such as increasing sales or something less direct like climbing the ranking of trusted providers within the industry.

Marketing plans are operational documents that get more attention because they are the day-to-day work that a company does to sell itself to the world. That said, a marketing plan would be meaningless without a message, a target market, and a goal — the core of every marketing strategy.

It takes a lot of time and effort to develop and maintain a marketing campaign that resonates with your intended audience. As a strategic thinker, however, the development of a marketing campaign takes even more consideration. After all, we're always searching for ways to gain the oh-so-important competitive edge.

There are times, though, when we all hit the proverbial wall. If you find yourself in that situation, then you may want to check out these fifteen marketing strategies that will spark your creative energy.

1) Partner with allies

Marketing partnerships have several benefits to push a marketing campaign. For starters, when you collaborate with someone else, you tend to deliver better content. On top of that, marketing partnerships are cheaper to create, see success more quickly, and expose your brand to a new audience.

For example, before being acquired by eBay, Half.com convinced the town of Halfway, Oregon, to change its name to Half.com in exchange for stock, Internet access, and other giveaways. The tactic gained a lot of attention from the textbook rental company. Another example was when Converse teamed up with Guitar Center to record music entitled "Rubber Tracks." The content was then used to create a series of YouTube videos that focused on the musicians.

2) Embrace user-generated content

According to a survey of 839 millennials, they spend "5.4 hours a day with content created by their peers. This represents 30 percent of their total media time and is rivaled only by all traditional media types combined (print, radio, and television, at 33 percent)." In the same survey, "Millennials reported that UGC is 20 percent more influential on their purchase decisions than other media."

You can achieve this by having customers share personal stories (Estee Lauder's international breast cancer action campaign), exchange ideas

(Salesforce's Idea Exchange), and by giving them the tools to make an ad for you (Nissan's VersaVid campaign that was shared on Instagram and Vine) or through humor (Doritos Roulette bags).

3) Collaborate with influencers

Another way to gain a new audience and extend brand awareness is by collaborating with the top influencers in your industry. The home improvement store Lowe's allowed "top designers and mom bloggers to take over its Instagram account for a few days at a time." By allowing these influencers to share inspirational content, Lowe's was able to tap into a new audience.

4) Help customers solve a problem

As perfectly stated on HubSpot, "You're in business because you provide solutions." Some of the ways you can help customers solve a problem are by creating how-to content, offering exclusives that make their lives easier, listening/responding to them or creating apps/tools.

You could also create a campaign as Orca Chevrolet did in Brazil. The company partnered with a local tow company and rescued stranded drivers by arriving in the new Orca. Not only did Chevy save the day, but it also gave drivers a chance to test drive the car.

5) **Let customers interact**

No matter the product or service you're offering, your customers want to interact with your company, or at least other customers. AMC, for example, created an online tool that allowed you to Mad Man Yourself. American Express connects small business owners and helpful resources through its OPEN Forum.

6) **Experiment with new channels and platforms**

Don't hesitate to try out new channels and platforms to promote your brand. As Clare McDermott, editor of Chief Content Officer magazine and owner of SoloPortfolio points out on the Content Marketing Institute, the Four Seasons introduced the PinPack. Go program on Pinterest. This was an industry-first campaign that allowed guests to co-curate a customer travel itinerary through a Pinterest board

7) Take a bite out of Apple

Apple deserves special mention mainly because it's a brand that has created an entire generation of lifelong advocates. How did they accomplish this? Remember when the iPod was introduced? Apple's now-iconic strategy involved empathy, focus, and impute when they used silhouettes of people enjoying the iPod. It may not have been the best MP3 player, but it created brand recognition that helped dominate the market.

8) Have some fun

You probably never heard of Dollar Shave Club until the company released that humorous YouTube video. The company continues to have its way with the shaving industry. Taco Bell and Old Spice are other examples of companies that are having fun with their marketing campaigns. Even campaigns you wouldn't expect are getting in on the action.

Caterpillar launched its "Built for It" campaign by having five Cat construction machines playing a giant game of Jenga.

9) Get employees involved

Let employees be your biggest champions and brand advocates. That's what happened with Caterpillar's "Built for It" campaign. The videos tapped into the allegiance of the brand, which motivated them to share the videos with friends and family.

10) Be a little weird

You don't always have to play it safe. Sometimes you want to think outside of the box and get a little weird. For example, to help launch the new radio station FM 96.3 in Glasgow, Scotland, the station placed empty guitar racks throughout the city. The hook? Each rack had a sign that read: "Free Air Guitar. Take One." It was unique and matched the brand perfectly - who hasn't played a little air guitar when listening to the radio?

11) Don't forget about the existing customers

It is important to obtain new customers if you want your business to grow, but don't forget about the customers you already have. As Belle Beth Cooper notes on the Buffer Blog, you could use the "upside-down funnel" approach. This could include making customers feel like they're part of an exclusive club, giving them something extra, and making them feel like VIPs.

12) Use big data to target customers

Big data is now helping retailers target specific customers. Red Roof Inn uses canceled flight information to send messages to stranded travelers. A pizza chain uses data to send out coupons to customers who are experiencing bad weather or power outages. In short, big data can be used to predict purchasing trends. With this information, you can get in touch with consumers before they search for your products or services.

13) Venture into the concrete jungle

You can still do a little offline marketing to create a buzz surrounding your product or service. For example, you could hire an artist to paint a mural (with permission, of course). You could also go the route of Citi Bike. Having bicyclists riding around with your logo or name is a clever way to grab attention. Another great example was when the Copenhagen Zoo shrink-wrapped city buses so that it appeared that they were squeezed by a giant boa constrictor.

14) Tap into nostalgia

Entrepreneur magazine shared an interesting discovery from the Journal of Consumer Research. The study found "that people who were asked to think about the past were willing to pay more for products than those who were asked to think about new or future memories; another experiment showed an increased willingness to give more money to others after recalling a nostalgic event." Maybe that's why brands like Coca-Cola, Calvin Klein, and Internet Explorer have launched campaigns that take Millennials back to the 90s.

15) Tell a cross-media story

Storytelling is one of the most effective methods of marketing. But how do you modernize it? Axe's "Susan Glenn" is a perfect example of a modern story that was shared across various media platforms. If you don't recall, Axe tapped into the memories of the girl who got away. Instead of just repacking the content, the story was told differently on different channels. There was also a 60-second film, an interactive billboard at Times Square, and unbranded memes.

Section One:

Marketing Strategy Definitions

Marketing strategies are used by businesses to promote their products and services. Let's have a look at the proper definition.

Marketing Strategy Definition

Marketing strategy is used by different companies to collaborate with their consumers. It is also employed to notify the customers about the features, specifications, and benefits of the company's products. It is focused on encouraging a target population to buy those specific products and services. The marketing strategies might be innovative or they can be previously tried or tested strategies. Effective marketing strategies help a company get ahead of the competition. They might be innovative or they can be previously tried or tested strategies.

Points to Ponder for Marketing

There are different types of marketing strategies available. You have to pick one as per your business requirements. Before choosing the right marketing strategy for your business, consider the following points.

1) Define the target population

Defining the target population is the main and most necessary step in choosing your marketing strategy. It gives the proper demographics which helps in selecting the most appropriate marketing plan for your business.

2) Test your audience

Create a hypothetical process of buying to test your audience. Once you know the buying behavior of your target audience, you can select a more appropriate marketing strategy.

3) Consider marketing strategies

Once you know the demographics - their knowledge, attitudes, and behaviors - you can select a more appropriate marketing strategy.

4) Evaluate those strategies

Once you have considered the marketing strategies and found the applicable ones, asses them, apply them, and evaluate them. This process must be for testing purposes and the most suitable and productive strategy must be applied.

Types of Marketing Strategies

There are different types of marketing strategies available. Picking up a marketing strategy includes analyzing the needs of your business, your target audience, and the specifications of your products.

The two main types of marketing strategy are:

Business to business (B2B) is the marketing of products to businesses or other organizations for use in the production of goods, for use in general business operations (such as office supplies), or resale to other consumers (such as a wholesaler selling to a retailer).

Business to consumer (B2C) marketing refers to the process of selling products and services directly between consumers who are the end-users of its products or services. Most companies that sell directly to consumers can be referred to as B2C companies

The most common form of marketing is business-to-consumer (B2C) marketing. Let's explore a bit more.

The following are the different types of marketing strategies available.

1) Paid advertising

This includes multiple approaches to marketing. It includes traditional approaches like TVCs and print media advertising. Also, one of the most well-known marketing approaches is internet marketing. It includes various methods like PPC (pay per click) and paid advertising.

2) Cause marketing

Cause marketing links the services and products of a company to a social cause or issue. It is also well known as cause-related marketing.

3) Relationship marketing

This type of marketing is focused on customer building, enhancing existing relationships with customers, and improving customer loyalty.

4) Undercover marketing

This type of marketing strategy focuses on marketing the product while customers remain unaware of the marketing strategy. It is also known as stealth marketing.

5) Word of mouth

This type relies on what impression you leave on people. It is traditionally the most important type of marketing strategy. Being heard is important in the business world. When you give quality services to customers, they'll likely promote you.

6) Internet marketing

This type is also known as cloud marketing. It usually happens over the Internet. All the marketing items are shared on the Internet and promoted on various platforms via multiple approaches.

7) Transactional marketing

Sales are particularly the most challenging work. Even for the largest retailers, selling is always tough, especially when there are high volume targets. However, with the new marketing strategies, selling isn't as difficult as it was. In transactional marketing, retailers encourage customers to buy with shopping coupons, discounts, and huge events. It increases the chances of sales and motivates the target audience to buy the promoted products.

8) Diversity marketing

This type caters to a diverse audience by customizing and integrating different marketing strategies. It covers different aspects like culture, beliefs, attitudes, views, and other specific needs.

9) Brand marketing

Companies, businesses, or individuals must always be observant of their public reputation. An online presence is important, but making sure the content is favorable is essential. This is why brand marketing is advantageous. The idea behind this method is to create content based on client testimonials. The concept most likely will not improve search results; nonetheless, it does have a positive impact on brand image. Beware, however, that when consumers research the brand, the results must be constructive. Any negative feedback will be detrimental. Do not mistake this kind of marketing for brand management, that is a whole other segment of business maintenance.

In Conclusion

Marketing strategies have made it much easier to promote products and services. They also limit the strategy to the target audience ensuring the proper advancement of the business.

Chapter Three:

What are Hashtags?

Remember the old days when symbols were something you used on a typewriter or dialed on a phone? Now with social media and the invention of smartphones, it has brought about a whole new meaning to communication. Today when using any social media platform, it's impossible to escape using some type of symbols like hashtags or emoticons. But in this section, we will be discussing just hashtags.

It's not surprising that you may be unfamiliar with how to use, or the meaning of, a hashtag. It's a relatively new concept unless you're part of the younger generation. We all know how our children migrate to electronics.

Once we explain "what" a hashtag is, you will most likely know "how" to use them. At first glance, the use of hashtags might seem confusing. But it's a powerful marking tool to engage your audience with literally no cost.

The concept started because of the demanding competition within social media platforms. If you want to stand out from the crowd, the user must create a unique approach to having their post seen. Hence, the reason for hashtags and emoticons. "The specific definition of the hashtag is a keyword or phrase preceded by the hash symbol (#), written within a post or comment to highlight and facilitate a search," WIXBlog.com. The idea is that the post can be indexed by the social network for anyone to locate even if they are not one of your followers. By increasing impressions, you essentially improve marketing goals.

With the use of hashtags, your social contacts are expanded to more than just your followers. Think of this as content-based marketing, similar to shopping on Amazon where it shows you recommended products in the same category as what you have chosen. It has the potential of reaching thousands of more users that could lead to customers or new followers.

One concept that must be observed: It can be tempting to use a simple word like #write, but with millions of posts each day, the chances of it being noticed are small. A better option would be a more specific hashtag such as #lovewriting. It will allow you to follow specific hashtags and people with similar interests. Give the tag some thought before posting.

Hashtags Have Three Categories

Content hashtags: As the title dictates, content hashtags pertain to your expertise, product, or service. They have the potential to greatly expand your brand.

Trending hashtags: A great way to capitalize on boosting your brand is using popular hashtags. But use caution; remember to analyze the word ahead of time and ask, "Will this tag increase my brand, or get lost in the millions of other posts each day?" The best trending hashtags are the ones that go viral; random moments about something funny, holidays, or spur-of-the-moment thoughts.

Brand-specific hashtags: If you choose to use a prevalent or generic hashtag, the posts may be lost in the shuffle. It's a good idea to create a unique word and be consistent. One great way to expand your brand is to get users to engage with incentives like discounts or free products. Plus, you can always test different hashtags to find out which ones get the best response, and no one is saying you must use only one hashtag.

One last word of caution: do not go overboard. Using hashtags to write an entire caption can defeat your agenda. Each channel has a specific number of hashtags allowed in each post. The last suggestion is only put hashtags next to a word with the most significance.

According to buffer social media research shows the best results on each one of these three channels. Below are a few of the top social site results:

- GETTR: One to two #s
- Parler: One to two #s
- GAB: One to Four #s
- Minds: One to Four #s
- MeWe: One to Four #s
- Clouthub: One to Four #s
- Telegram: One to Three #s

GETTR

Hashtagging on GETTR can have a major impact when it comes to follower count. It can be used with general and/or non-specific hashtags. If general hashtag words are used that are prominent, such as #creative, #events, #TIFF, it is more likely that tweets will reach beyond your follower list.

GETTR hashtags encourage people to take part in conversations with the same topic, and users to engage with one another even if they are not following each other. While hashtagging on GETTR can help social media presence, using long and wordy hashtags, like #bestcoffeeshopintheworld, in a post can damage your presence, as hashtags are used to increase search results and engage with others. In addition to long hashtags, using too many hashtags in one post can also be harmful to social media presence. If the tweet is filled with more hashtags than content, it will provide evidence that the business or individual is desperate and certainly dilutes the message being conveyed.

Parler

As with GETTR, using hashtags on Parler can help engage with more than just your followers. Hashtags on Instagram give "audiences an organic way to discover branded content through the topics and forums that interest them," according to Jenna MacDonald. Community engagement is a good way to build a brand, whereas hashtags allow users to find specific members of the community to interact with. The main concept is to increase presence on social media through other avenues besides gaining followers (MacDonald, 2017).

Parler hashtags can assist with building a bigger audience. A great way to expand your presence is using the same hashtags of the audience that is interacting with your posts or to follow the same topics. Avoid using hashtags on photos; they function better added to the input section while creating the post.

LinkedIn

It is a common misbelief that hashtags should be used on every platform, but that is not the case. As an example, hashtags are less effective on LinkedIn. The use of hashtags on LinkedIn should conservative. A better way to improve impressions or engagement is by posting quality content.

In conclusion, if you have not chosen to use hashtags on social media posts it may be time to put the action to good use. The use of hashtags seems to be a growing craze that could benefit any business, company, or individual looking to improve their online presence.

Chapter Four:

Social Media and Email Marketing make great partners

As social media continues to progress and become more popular around the globe, some businesses think email marketing has fallen by the wayside. But, it's just the opposite. According to Neil Patel, 85% of adult internet users have and use email regularly. That outranks surfing the web and social media which shows only 17%. Now, imagine if you combined the two marketing options? Anytime a business owner can intermingle marketing strategies with a cross-platform, their results will improve dramatically.

The number of consumers that make buying choices based on a single medium is limited. Therefore, marketers should never focus all their time on one channel. Multiple advertising options correlate with buyers' natural rhythms. So, let's talk about how you can combine multiple mediums to improve business and reach a greater audience.

Shareaholic states, “Facebook is the number one referral traffic source for websites.” Websites like Buzzfeed get most of their website traffic from social media.

But, for the marketing plan to work, you must continue using both outlets equally. The strategies remain the same: quality tagline, magnetic subject lines, etc.

If you’re a business owner, chances are you’ve already considered using social media marketing to help get the word out about your business.

In fact, many conservative small business owners are switching to sites such as LinkedIn, GETTR, Clouthub, Gab, Minds, MeWe, and Telegram, to help grow their businesses. And if you are still standing on the social sidelines, there’s never been a better time to get started.

Below are ten reasons social media marketing could benefit any business, company, or individual, according to Constant Contact.

1) **Social media helps get the word out:** First and foremost — social media does, in fact, help get the word out about your business.

But even more important than the exposure, it provides you with the opportunity to grow relationships with your target audience. Your fans, followers, and connections are people who know your organization, have likely done business with you in the past, and will be most likely to tell their friends about you.

2) **Social media is popular:** You don't need to be a dedicated reader of tech blogs or an expert in online marketing to know that social media is popular among consumers.

   According to the Pew Research Center, 69 percent of American adults use social networks, which means that social media will touch nearly every customer that walks through your door.

   For most small businesses, Telegram — which has 550 monthly active users — is the jumping-off point for getting started with social media marketing.

   With its extensive reach and dynamic functionality, there are very few businesses that couldn't benefit from having a presence on Telegram.

Conservatives backing President Trump understand the election malfeasance of 2020 and beyond, sparked a migration to alternative social media sites that refrain from censoring users.

The shift has boosted favorites like Parler, Gab, and Rumble which have rejected the approach of Facebook and Twitter in labeling and limiting free speech.

According to Sensor Tower, "Parler, founded in 2018, saw more than 3.3 million downloads from Apple and Google marketplaces since November 3 to reach 7.3 million installs globally."

Large gains were also seen for other conservative-friendly services such as OANN, RSBN-- which Trump himself endorsed -- as well as MeWe and Bitchute.

Fox Business TV host Maria Bartiromo, in recent days, announced she would be leaving Twitter, with a tweet saying, "I'll be posting on Parler bc as you know I won't tolerate censorship." Bartiromo and others called on their Twitter followers to migrate to Parler.

3) **Social media is cost-effective:** As more social networks add algorithms that filter what users see in their news feeds, your organic content may get lost in the shuffle. Take advantage of the low-cost advertising features offered by social networks to promote your content and special offers.

   Most social media advertising is cheaper than traditional advertising, so you don't have to spend a lot of money to reach more people, increase your audience, and grow your business.

   The next section will show business owners how to leverage these two channels to improve audience impressions.

4) **Social media reaches all ages and demographics:** social media defies age barriers. A Pew Research Center study found that 69 percent of US adults are using social networks.

While much of that percentage is between 18-29, a substantial amount is attributed to other ages that use social media as well, including 34% of Americans 65 and older. So, no matter how young or old your target audience may be, chances are most of them are already logging on and waiting for you to get started.

5) **Social media encourages two-way communication:** social media gives you the power to learn more about your audience, their interests, and collect feedback.

   Ask your customers to share their thoughts, questions, and ideas to get to know them better. You can respond just as fast, without having to pick up the phone or worry the customer isn't seeing your response.

6) **Social media users are active:** One thing you have to know about social media users is that when they say they are on social media; they are really on social media.

Social media users in the US check their accounts 17 times a day, according to an Informate Mobile Intelligence report. While a customer may visit your store once a week, they could see your social media posts in their feed multiple times during the week.

7) **Social media lets you share A LOT about your business:** social media sites are becoming the go-to place for consumers who want to learn more about a business. That's because these sites allow businesses to offer the most up-to-date information about anything from products, services, or upcoming events.

   Also, much of your activity and profiles on social media sites can be made public, meaning they can be indexed by search engines — one more way to make sure your business or organization comes up as the answer when someone is searching for a solution to a problem.

8) **Social media is perfect for customer service:** Providing stellar customer service is likely already a top priority for your small business.

But along with the two-way communication that social media provides, it also offers a unique opportunity to step up your customer service game and provide instant gratification to your target audience.

This will allow you to showcase just how much you care about providing a memorable experience and will ensure that no customer inquiry goes unnoticed. And by monitoring social media for customer feedback and offering a response, you can drive real business results. Businesses that engage with customer service requests via social media earn 20-40 percent more revenue per customer, according to Bain and Company.

9) **Social media can make a big difference for your email marketing:** social media has completely changed the game when it comes to how small businesses think of email marketing. Sharing your email newsletter across your social networks can open your content up to a whole new audience and generate the type of buzz you've been looking for.

Not only that, but you can also use sites like Gab to attract more readers by including a Join My Mailing List link right on your page.

Together, these two powerful tools have reshaped the marketing landscape and have leveled the playing field for small businesses trying to better connect with current customers and reach new audiences for their business.

10) **Social media is everywhere:** Today, more than half of all Americans are smartphone users, and more and more businesses are offering mobile-friendly experiences. The benefit of the increased presence of mobile activity in our daily lives is huge for small businesses.

    The most major social networks, such as Facebook, Twitter, Pinterest, and Instagram, are losing users by the thousands due to censorship. Alternate media is growing rapidly, as these companies bypass the first amendment.

However, the upcoming popular social media sites still allow customers to connect with their favorite sites wherever they are. These users aren't just sharing updates from their own lives, they're searching for businesses, products, and services, and connecting with brands through their social channels.

Having a social media presence that's accessible via mobile can improve the chances of your business getting found when someone is searching for a place to eat or a product to buy while on the go (Collier, 2019).

According to a Constant Contact survey, small businesses that use multiple channels in conjunction with email reported: more customer engagement (73 percent), more new customers (57 percent), more website traffic (54 percent), more revenue (40 percent), and more referrals (39 percent).

Social media and email marketing are a team meant to benefit each other.

Connecting with your customers on major social media channels is a great way to build relationships and raise awareness for your business. But the real power of social media comes from integrating it with your other marketing channels — like email marketing. While many businesses will still have to use Facebook, Twitter, Instagram or YouTube accessibility to email integration is slowly becoming more convenient.

1) **Put a brand before the subscriber:** Upload your subscriber list on all major social media sites. The consumer can see your business in a real-time setting. One of the biggest challenges a company faces is building trust with its clients. When subscribers can interact with your business in a social setting, it improves brand image. Then, make sure your posts are solving a pain problem. How can your company help with an issue?
2) **Social media can grow an email list:** Lead generations can increase a subscriber list. Ads can be sent to users who've sent a message to your profile page within the last year. Collect the email and you can follow up later to see if they have received your message and whether they are interested in your product.

3) **Connect with your subscribers on social media:** Once you have uploaded your subscriber list to the major social media sites, it's important to connect with them. A few ways to interact might be:
    - Contact about missed messages in their Inbox.
    - Re-connect with subscribers who stopped opening emails.
    - Follow-up on future sales, or assist to help complete a project.
        - Plan a sale for specific groups of people, who like your company, or potential clients.
4) **Test email marketing strategies on social media:** The best way to get an idea of your marketing plan is to run some trials. When you have determined the response, adjust accordingly to increase response. Once you are satisfied with the outcome, create an email blast.

Marketing can be challenging, but it is a necessary evil that cannot be ignored. Below are some resources to help you with this task:

- Social Share: promote emails on social media
- Use Social Buttons: it makes it easier for contacts to locate your pages. When creating any post, make sure users can contact your business easily. Provide a direct link.
- Grow Your List: social media can be used to gather the names directly into your contact list

- Social Media Calendars: The best way to improve a social media presence is to use a schedule calendar. However, using alternate media is not available for scheduling posts, currently.
- Create Posts from Email Blasts: Posts will appear on social platforms and educate followers. When users click the post, it takes them directly to the email.
- Invite Contacts to Your Profile Page
- Add a Sign-up Form

Marketing any business has its challenges under the best of circumstances. But with commitment, strategy, and planning, the process is much simpler. One of the best practices is to study the market and learn your type of client. Then, focus your energy on reaching that type of consumer. Remember, whatever you focus on grows, either good or bad. People can read and feel the intentions behind your marketing, so keep it honest.

Chapter Five:

GAB Personal/Upgraded Accounts

Gab is an American-based alternative media social networking service widely known for its conservative community/user base. Launched in 2017, similar to Facebook as it is also a microblogging platform but with a twist.

Steps To Use Gab

Go to the official website of GAB (gab.com) through your browser on a desktop or device. Create an account, if you do not have one already. Click on the 'Sign Up' option present in the upper right corner of your screen.

Once the account is created a welcome to GAB message gives the latest news. Consider it an overview of what to expect.

Using GAB

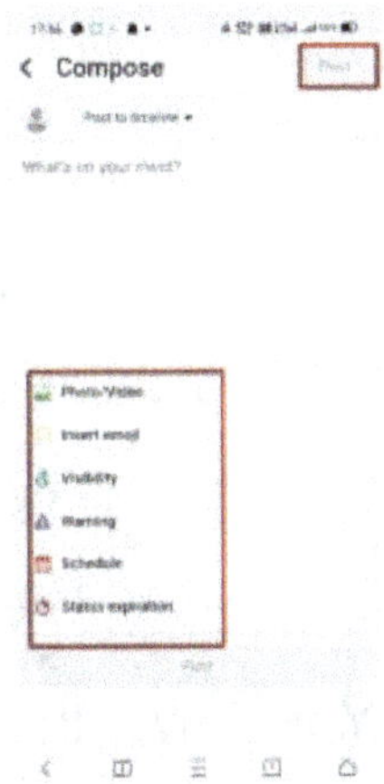

The initial step is to complete your profile; click the circle area to upload your profile photo, then add a cover photo. After completing the process, click on the 'next' present at the bottom right.

GAB's Profile Section

The next phase is looking for people or groups to join and follow. Once you've joined all your desired groups then you'll have the option to publish a post directly from there or you can do that later from the home page.

GAB's Group Section

On the homepage, at the top right corner click on your profile photo and select Profile from the options. You can see bookmarks, timeline, photos, videos, and comments. It also shows the number of followers, likes posts, and who's following you. If you want more info, please follow the link, How to create an account on GAB?

To create a gab (publishing blog) look at the right side and click on the ‘create gab’ icon. You can write about your opinions, plus there are several other options to add other attachments.

- Adding a photo
- Adding an emoji
- Sensitive information
- Add Hashtags

You have the option to make your post public or private. In case you use GAB routinely, there’s an option to schedule your post if you have an upgraded account. After creating the post just click on ‘publish’.

GAB's Profile Options

Go to the homepage click on your profile photo; tap the 'help' option. The section allows you to ask or seek assistance related to the gab.

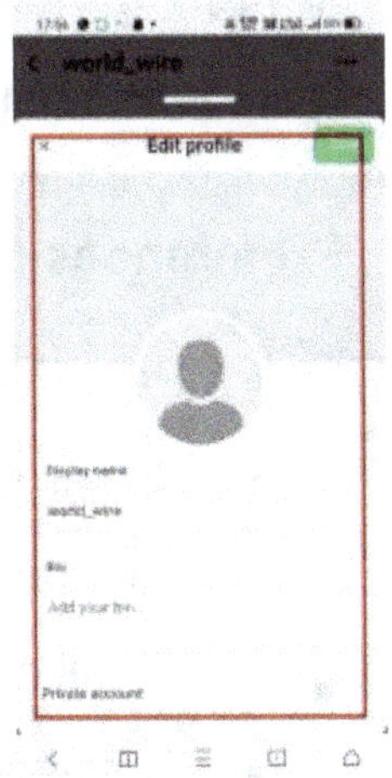

Under settings include these options:

- Edit Your Profile
- Edit Your Display Name
- Profile Photo
- Bio

Accounts can be locked to manually approve followers or mark it as a bot account. Click Save when finished.

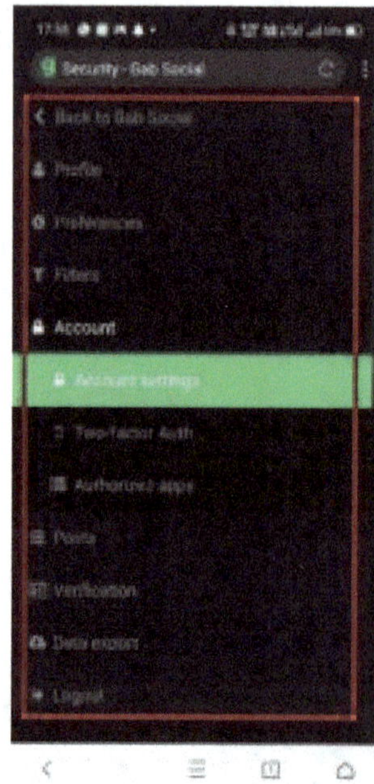

Preferences Option

- Post Privacy
- Preferred Languages
- Two-factor authorization
- Email address
- Password reset

GAB's Settings Menu and Its Components

The homepage includes an Explore option. The tab includes the most popular posts;

- Popular news stories
- Breaking news headlines
- GAB stock

Success Tips to Grow Your Business with Gab

Create your Gab Ads account quickly on grow.gab.com

1. Log In/Connect with Gab
2. Complete The Form
3. Submit And Wait for Approval from The Support Team

1. Know The GAB Community

- Align your message with community values and interests
- Build your brand with consistent messaging across your profile, groups, images, or ads timing
- Any Marketing plan should include relationship Building

Key Values:

- Conservatism
- Free Speech
- Family
- Christian
- Trust
- Engagement

2. **Know Gab Features**

- Create your marketing plan by aligning messaging (profile, groups, ads, videos)
- Build distribution channels with gab's relational networking tools (follows, groups, networking)
- Explore all the features available (gab ads, GabTV, groups, private chats, Gab Pay. (Market Place is coming soon)
- Spend time exploring the site daily to learn how gab features work

3. **Best Practices**

- Consider a separate business Gab account
- GAB Pro subscribers may utilize enhanced features (account verification, GabTV channel uploads, Pro feed)

- Define metrics to measure business success, gauge what works for your business
- Keep it fresh with high-quality content, engagement, and customer feedback with successes
- Minimize spammy posting behavior as followers will see all posts
- Create demand by posting interest related groups, use coupons or discounts
- Build a network to increase reach with follows, groups, engagement
- Check out other successful GAB business pages for ideas
- Design a profile/group/channel to become a destination that people want to revisit

Section Two:

GAB Advertising

Creating Ads on Gab (Advertisers)

Gab has developed and launched an ads service that enables users to create and manage advertising for businesses on the GAB platform.

Marketing Campaign

Begin by mapping the campaign. Consider GAB's tools, features, and the community's culture to optimize

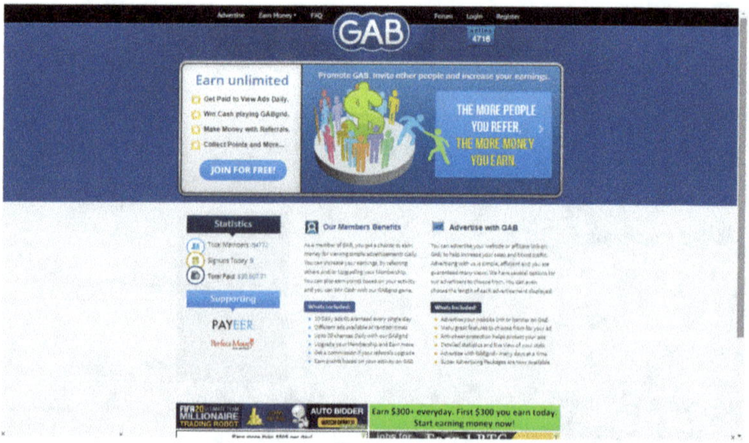

message and reach. Benchmark successful advertisers to use what applies to your business.

Building a business on GAB will be rewarding. The early ad testers found high levels of customer interest and increased sales when using GAB's ads.

Helpful Links

- https://help.gab.com/article/what-is-gab-com
- https://help.gab.com/article/basics-social-engagement-network
- https://help.gab.com/article/business-account-gab-ads

Apply for a new Gab Ad Account: https://grow.gab.com

The process includes a short application to help understand the platform. The form will ask for a business name, URL, email address, monthly advertising budget, and a short description of your products/services.

Create First Ad Campaign

After account approval, return to the site to 'Sign In'. On the Ad Dashboard, you can manage the GAB Ad account.

Set up Campaign

Select the green button to begin a new campaign. All ads created with your GAB Ad account will be a unique campaign with its budget, duration, and artwork.

Examples of campaigns include: showcasing your products/services, a seasonal sale, special promotion, announcement, etc.

Image Sizes

- Brand image: (1:1, square)
- Ad image: 16:9 to 1:1 (jpg, jpeg, png)

As you fill in the form, the preview image will auto-update with new information, creating a unique ad preview. Upon completion, the new campaign will be sent to the gab team for final review and uploading to the site.

Manage Ad Account with the Dashboard. After campaign approval, the dashboard will adjust with updated analytics. Dashboard metrics include your daily/total spend, clicks, views, CTR (click-thru rate), and CPC (cost/click). Multiple ad campaigns can be sorted by attribute. Ads can be paused, edited then restart.

Billing

Funds can be added by clicking the 'add funds' button, found on the Ad Overview page.

The account should be kept in a positive balance. Accounts with a longtime outstanding balance may be disabled until the outstanding balance is paid.

Terms of Service https://gab.com/about/tos

Chapter Six:

Using MeWe

MeWe started a few years ago; testing began in 2015. However, the network didn't start its growth until 2018, where it reached 2.5 million.

Considered anti-Facebook, the network prides itself on not censoring free speech. It has similar features and feels like Facebook, however, Minds is also an alternative social network to Twitter. Many people have either been banned or left due to censorship.

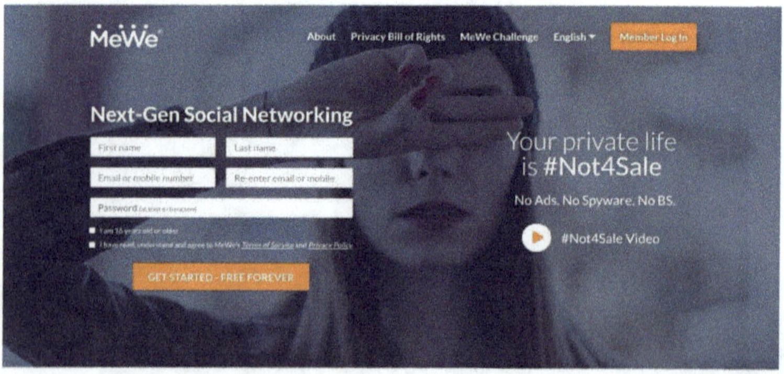

Personal Page vs. Business Page on MeWe

To get started, sign up as a personal page.

- Banner sizes are best 945×320 pixels.
- The profile picture is best at 250×250

If you want a business page, you can purchase one for $1.99 per month. They make money off a subscription-based model vs. an ad model as Facebook or GAB.

MeWe is set up with a search option on the home screen.

Hashtags on MeWe

Hashtags help, just like they do on most other social media networks today. Hashtags work best when someone searches and finds posts via a hashtag. But, keep the hashtags to one or two, well thought out words.

MeWe Groups

In 2018, it was reported that MeWe had over 90,000 groups on the social media site. Some groups are private but most are public.

The number of groups gives ample choices to join in on topics and spread your message. You may also start your own group.

MeWe Chats

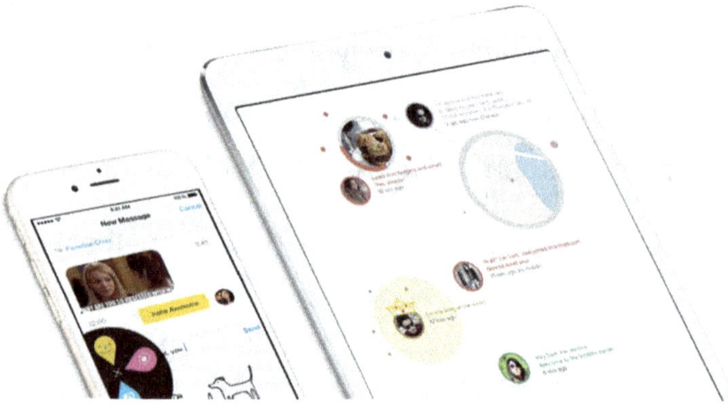

The chat feature allows you to chat with groups or individuals on the platform. It can be used on a mobile or desktop. You can stop notifications to see them vs. hear them.

Some chat features include:

- Photos
- Videos
- Dual-Camera MeWe's
- Emojis
- Stickers
- Doodles

- Files
- GIFs
- Voice messages

Private Posts

Private posts are only shared with contacts, like a messenger. The chat can also be deleted at any time.

On mobile, you can share disappearing content and your location in chats.

Notifications Tab

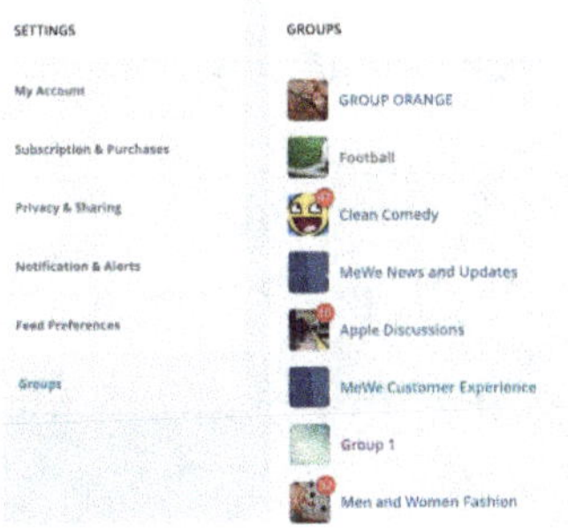

The notification sent alters upon receiving messages or comments on posts. They are located on the upper right-hand side of your desktop.

On a mobile device, a red dot will appear for new messages or notifications. Please note that the notifications tab on a mobile is on the bottom of your screen.

Stories Feature

On a mobile device, you can share stories on the network, the same as most other social media platforms. They are vertical size images. Similarly, you can share with contacts, close friend's list, or the public.

Stories disappear within 24 hours. Hence, people love them, as they fear missing out.

Photos or videos can also be used for your story feature. Some emojis and text are available. Slideshow stories are also available.

On mobile, stories posted by your contacts and the pages, you follow appear at the top of the home screen. However, on the desktop, stories appear on the right side of your screen, right below new posts. By clicking on the story, you can reply or comment.

Paid Subscriptions

Several options are available or use the platform for free.

MeWe does not offer ads, but rather, their money is made from subscriptions.

A premium subscription includes:

- Video Journals for Your Stories
- Unlimited Voice + Video Calling
- And Unlimited Custom Emojis + Stickers*
- Unlimited Custom Themes

- 100GB of MeWe Cloud Storage
- and a Premium Profile Badge
- A Value of Over $30 per Month FREE for 30 Days. Then Only $4.99 per Month. Furthermore, it is RISK-FREE as you can cancel anytime!

MeWe Share Button with Shareaholic

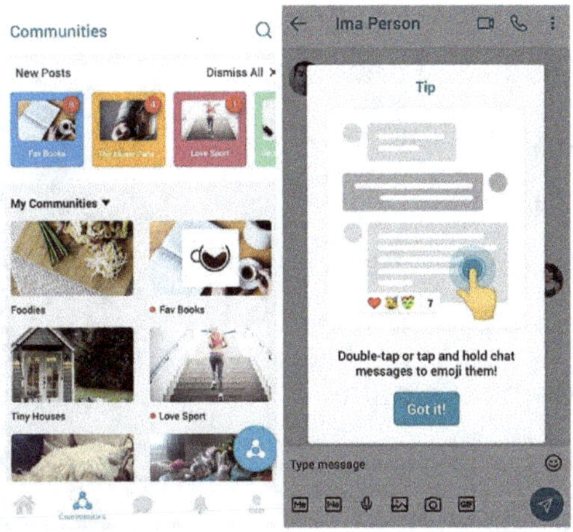

MeWe has a button to use on blogs or websites if you use the Shareaholic plugin. Other share buttons are also available.

Chapter Seven:

Using Minds

Minds is a new social media platform built on free speech. Member's data is not tracked or collected.

The Minds platform has launched its cryptocurrency on the Ethereum test net. By interacting with other users, you can earn tokens for the exchange.

What is Minds.com?

As a real alternative to Twitter and Facebook. The site was created in many ways as a response to the recent bouts of censorship and data mining on other social media websites. Sites like Facebook and Twitter, etc.

track everything and then sell all your information to advertisers.

In response to this blatant censorship, Minds.com was created with the intent that no legally protected speech would be censored or subverted. The site itself has no specific political bias, and opinions from all sides of the spectrum are welcomed and encouraged. Additionally, Minds.com does not engage in active user tracking or in selling personal data to advertisers. More so, Minds.com is largely immune to the types of major data breaches seen by Facebook with the recent Cambridge Analytica scandal.

A few other new social media pioneers join Minds.com that focus on or at least a connection to the cryptocurrency world, including Steemit, Yours.org, and Gab.ai. The goals of these websites are often not to replace existing social media networks, but rather offer an alternative.

Bill Ottman is the CEO of Minds.com, who was interviewed by Tucker Carlson on Fox News. He is a proponent of free speech.

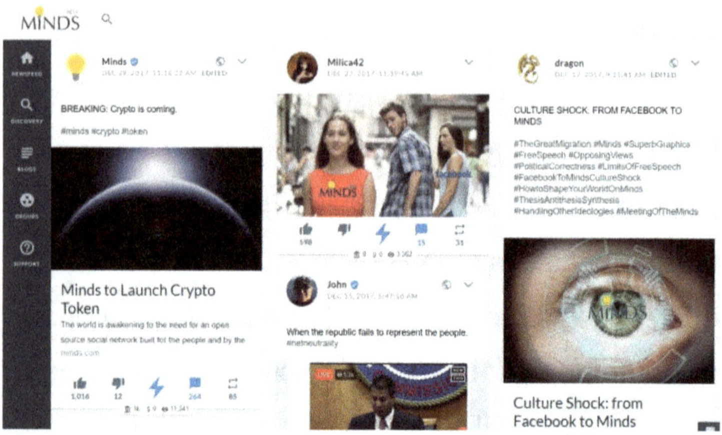

Using Minds

Once you have created an account. Users provide a phone number, but the data is never sold. Instead, only used to prevent spam bot sign-ups.

Once your username and password are set, you can start earning cryptocurrency rewards for using the site, as well as for posting messages, writing blogs, sharing videos and pictures.

Earning Minds Tokens

Tokens can be earned by performing almost any normal activity on a social media site. For instance, creating a post, liking or disliking something, sharing a photo, uploading a video, or writing a blog post. By reminding a post, it can be re-shared. Earning tokens on the site is so simple that even just logging into your profile page on a browser or mobile app counts as a check-in and can earn you cryptocurrency.

How Rewards Are Determined

All actions earn different points. These points are added to your daily contribution total. Simple actions like checking your feed or uploading something are only worth a few points. Conversely, contributing content like sharing a link or writing a blog post is worth more.

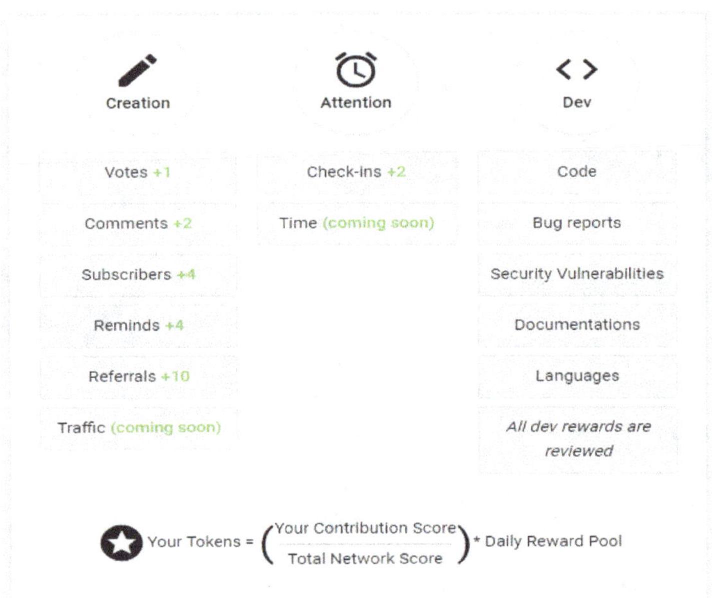

The points are totaled daily, and the user is given a percentage based on the number of points earned compared to everyone else on the site.

Users are given a daily token payout equal to the total amount given to the network each day, divided by the percentage of points you contributed. In other words, if you contribute several actions on a slow day, you would get more tokens than if you contributed the same amount on a busy day. In tests with the site, doing at least a few actions each day would get somewhere between 0.1 and 0.03 tokens per day. Below are the calculations of the test done on Minds.com.

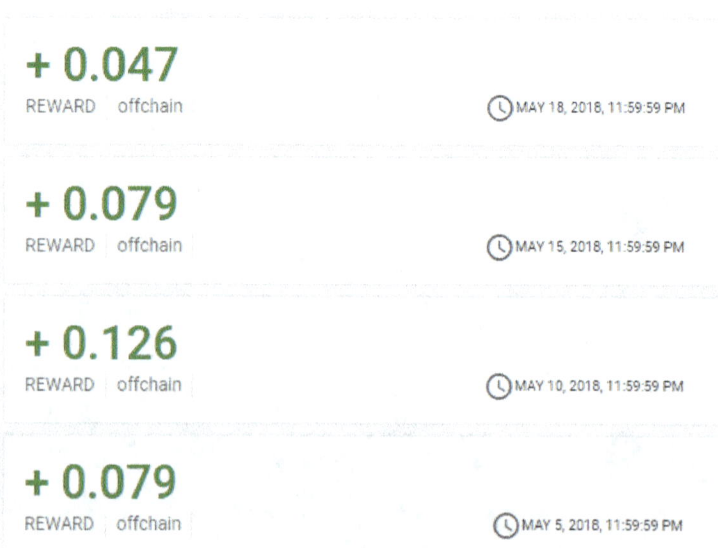

Minds Token

Post videos, blogs, images, and statuses. Message and video chat securely with groups or directly with friends. Discover great content through trending feeds and hashtags.

Earn tokens for daily contributions and use them to upgrade your channel, boost content for more reach, and support other creators.

You can also receive direct payments in USD, Bitcoin, and Ether from fans, or upgrade your account to launch a website and get paid for the traffic you drive.

Currently, Minds.com tokens can be used to boost any post or content shared on the site. Boosting is basically like promoting or advertising your content with high priority to all interested users. One token can be used to boost a post for up to 1000 impressions. An impression means your post will appear in the feed of at least 1000 people. It does not, however, mean a 1000 people will click through and read your blog post or link.

The great part is, if you post interesting enough content and boost it, you can actually earn back the token you spent to boost the post, and perhaps even earn a positive net profit if your content was well-received. Building subscribers that like and remind your posts can also increase earnings on the platform.

The site even offers a Patreon-style feature, where fans can unlock premium content by directly sending you tokens through a process called a wire. Additionally, token wires can be sent as a tip of sorts through the network without having to pay transaction fees.

Conclusion

Minds.com is a highly-polished platform and easy-to-use. It offers essentially all the features of Facebook, YouTube, and Twitter all together in one neat package. However, without boosting posts, the content will only get a handful of views. Boosting is quick and easy, though, in many cases free (assuming you use tokens earned instead of bought). These levels out the playing field to some degree.

Minds.com is a work in progress, but with its values of free speech put front and center, as well as its innovative integration of cryptocurrency, Minds.com could be an interesting and fully functional alternative to the overly intrusive and highly censorial platforms that we have today.

Chapter Eight:

Using LinkedIn? (censors)

Disclaimer – LinkedIn does censor, however it can be a valuable tool for building business connections.

What's Does Your Profile Say About You?

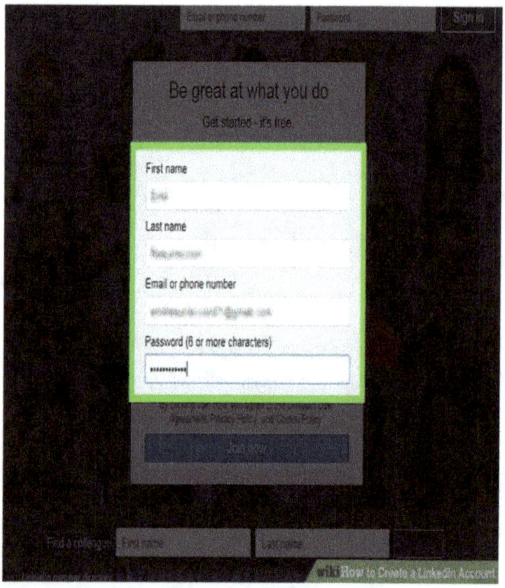

LinkedIn is considered the best option for the professional crowd. It is based more on networking resources, hiring, and finding job placement, gathering sales leads, and real-time industry news. But a word of caution: the platform is less user-friendly. It may even seem daunting; however, we are here to help you over that hurdle. Below are some steps for maximizing your profile:

1) **Complete your profile page:** Include all important details. Remember, an incomplete profile does not look professional.
2) **Emphasize your expertise:** Set up an image of professionalism, it puts you in the expert category.
3) **Create a call to action:** Write a precise call to action directive to explain your profession, something like see my website for further information. Make it clear and detailed; no one can read your mind.
4) **Always, always include a professional photo:** You can go to a local photographer and have high-quality pics done for a minimal charge. Selfies are not a preferred method.
5) **Optimize profile searches:** There are millions of people searching on LinkedIn, so your profile should be easily found. Do some research on the best keywords to give you the best chance of expanding a brand.
6) **Consistent posting:** Not only does posting help engagement, but it also improves organic SEO optimization.

7) **Create and actively participate in groups:** Networking is still one of the best marketing tools. Choose 2 or 3 of the biggest topics within your genre and discuss the topics with others.
8) **Be conscious about your connections:** LinkedIn is a professional platform; it's not Facebook. Some people will examine your profile for people with whom you associate. Spammers are a real issue on social media.
9) **Personalize messages:** Enable followers to connect with your message or brand.
10) **Learn/understand and follow trending content tools:** LinkedIn offers a tool to show content trends and allows you to weed out unwanted information.

Build Your Network

Once the specifics of setting up your profile are complete, it is time to start building a network. However, LinkedIn connections are vastly different than other platforms. The basis was designed for the professional networker. Therefore, be mindful of who you are accepting into your connection list.

Best options for connecting: Sending invitations on LinkedIn must be done with a high degree of professionalism. The clientele basis was founded for the businessman or woman. When creating a request take the time to explain your brand and why you are interested in connecting with that person.

Join the conversation: Many users get stuck once they build their network because they fail to join in on conversations. When building your brand, show off your knowledge, engage with other posts that pertain to your expertise.

What to share: The way someone presents themselves is very important. Start with sharing some newsworthy articles that relate to your area of expertise. If you have a blog or content that is produced by your company, use it to create a post that people can engage with. According to Constant Contact, "sharing it on your profile will help get it in front of people that have a vested interest in your industry and will be more likely to comment or share. Even better – use LinkedIn's Publisher feature to share your blog post. Publisher will give that article visibility in the feeds of your followers and will add it to your profile as an article" (Pinkham, 2019).

Unadvisable posts: As stated above, LinkedIn is a business professional social platform, so uploading pictures of your kids, funny jokes, reality TV news, sports rants, political rants, complaints about your boss, what you had for breakfast, what you want for lunch, your favorite type of ice cream ... Can you see where this is leading? Create a personal website on another platform to share stuff that pertains to your private life, but if your business is titled with a real name, for example, Lizzy McNett, then you must be cautious of everything that is posted. A quick Google search can tell a completely different story.

Explore the platform: LinkedIn has a multitude of outlets to share your brand with the community, such as the Work Tab.

LinkedIn Groups: These are sections that connect like-minded peers centered around a single topic.

Additional options:

- Slideshare houses presentations
- Infographics
- Documents, and more

Users can search for information on industry topics, bookmark slides they want to save in a clipboard, and upload their presentations to share with their peers.

Seven Qualities to Assist in Creating Authority on LinkedIn

Admittedly, LinkedIn may not be the most entertaining platform on the social media market; nonetheless, it is the most useful for expanding your business. At first glance, LinkedIn can be intimidating, but with some planning and practice, it will become a valuable tool for expanding your brand.

1) Who has viewed your profile: A great feature provided by LinkedIn to analyze is the profile? It provides insight into people who have viewed your profile for the last 90 days. The tool can be used to optimize your profile for the right audience.

   The tool allows users to look at the name, headline, location, industry, and how the people found you. Plus, users can view what keywords they were using, their title, and more. Stats can provide awareness of how your profile is perceived by the public.

2) **Your profile:** One of the most important tools of any platform is the profile section. The important areas to make you stand out are linking to visual examples of your work in your LinkedIn profile summary and job experience sections. Once that is completed, add documents, photos, links, videos, or presentations.

3) **Your headline:** Under your name is a great place to introduce yourself to followers or protentional clients. Write a compelling headline to grab attention.

4) **Connections' activity:** This tool is a great advantage for anyone looking to get an insight into their connections, or gain some ideas to give their profile a facelift. Plus, great conversations can be started by gaining a better sense of people's personalities, interests, needs, and concerns.

5) **Groups:** This area can open the door to meet new people, ideas, and gain resources

for your business. They offer a platform to discuss industry trends and news, post job openings, ask for opinions, and share expertise.

6) **Publisher:** This tool is an excellent way to connect with followers in a long-form format, outside of the limited post on your regular feed. Publisher allows users to get a more in-depth look at your professional thoughts. The section is searchable on or off LinkedIn. Plus, Publisher offers the ability to manage comments, edit and delete posts, view stats, and tag.

7) **LinkedIn app:** There's not much else to say in this section, except that you can get the app from Google Play or iTunes.

Writer's Publishing House

We provide exclusive features along with the following guidelines:

- Social Media Marketing
- Cost-Effective Marketing Resources

Online marketing is the action of advertising and marketing the products or services of a business over the internet. Advertising relies upon websites or emails to reach the intended users, combined with e-commerce to facilitate business transactions.

Social Media Development & Training - We will manage your social media marketing or train your marketing staff. Do you need a social media strategy or social media calendar we got you covered?

Email Marketing (Constant Contact Certified) - Do you have an Email Marketing system in place? We can help you set up and activate your Constant Contact 60-day free trial.

Local SEO and Reputation Marketing- Writer's Publishing House Social Media Marketing helps manage the public facts about your brand across the popular local directories' consumers search online.

Drive more search traffic to your business. Local SEO increases web traffic, leads, and sales from local visitors – If you're a local company, getting web visits and leads from users in a different city, state, or country won't do anything to build your business. With local SEO, you increase traffic from consumers in your specific service areas, which means you'll get a higher visit-to-sale rate.

Outsource Marketing- Our Services include Marketing Strategy, Content Strategy, Branding & Graphic Design, Collateral Development, Video Development, Digital Media, Ghost Writing,

Translation, Website Design, Strategic Communications, and Remote Staffing.

Content Strategy- We can create your business social media toolkits, Social Media Calendars, and develop all your content for all your social media sites

Strategic Communications- Let us promote your brand through events, promotions, social media ads, press releases.

Branding & Graphic Design- We have a team of Creative Designers that develop anything that you can imagine.

Learn more at ww.writerspublishinghouse.com

Chapter Nine:

Using Telegram

Telegram was launched in 2013 by brothers Nikolai and Pavel Durov. It is a registered American LLC. In October 2021, Telegram gained over 70 million new users. The platform currently has over 55.2 million daily users; ranked at 7th on apps downloaded across iOS and Android.

According to Telegram founder Pavel Durov, "25 million new users joined Telegram during a 72-hour surge in January 2021, which equates to about 8.33 million new sign-ups per day. And more than 100 million new users started using Telegram in January alone."

In fact, Telegram's user base has been growing at a rate of more than 40% each year since its launch in 2013. Telegram is a free speech platform with no censorship.

Telegram has become one of the most popular messaging apps available for both phones and desktops. The plethora of features makes it an instant hit. Option includes:

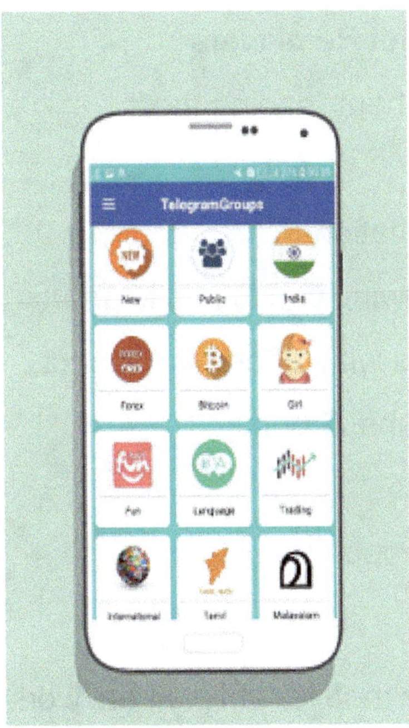

Tips and tricks to build followers on Telegram

- Use Hashtag
- Edit Sent Messages
- Send Silent or Scheduled Messages
- Send Self Destructing message.
- Select part of the message
- Send images without loss in quality.
- Add sticker to images before sending them.
- Edit Videos before sending
- Polls and Quiz Mode
- Saved Messages & Set Reminders
- Preview Message without reading them
- Create Chat Folders
- Lock Chats and application
- Stop People from allowing you to add to groups.
- Use multiple accounts with different numbers.
- Find Nearby People and Group
- Slow Mode for Groups
- Pin Messages in a Group
- Telegram Themes

Some options only work on a mobile, while others work on a desktop.

Hashtags on Telegram

Hashtags allow for faster search. One of the biggest problems in any messenger app is finding a particular conversation. Telegram solves it by using #hashtags. So, if you add #expenses in one of your conversations, then tapping on the hashtag will reveal all the conversations that contain the hashtag.

Edit Sent Messages

Telegram allows anyone to edit any error(s) in the sent message. The changes can be made for up to two days. Users can also see the original messages.

To edit any message, on mobile long-press on it, and on the desktop, right-click and choose to edit the message. It will open the text message, once you change, hit Enter.

Send Silent or Scheduled Messages

Whenever a message is sent, it goes instantly but can be sent silently or at a fixed time. Silent messages ensure the person is not notified, while the scheduled message will ensure you never forget to send the message.

Schedule Silent Message Telegram

To send a silent message, long-press the send button using a mobile, while on desktop make a right-click, and choose one of the options.

Secret Chat or Self-Destructing message

In case you don't want a message forwarded, it can be set to automatically delete.

On mobile devices only, tap on the contact, and then on the three-dot menu, select Start Secret Chat. For the conversation to start, the person will have to join the chat.... once he or she is here, you can send messages. To set up a self-destruct timer, tap on the menu, tap on the option and set up a time.

Secret messages block screenshots, forwards, and delete data once you choose to delete them.

Select Part of the Message

While it is easy on the desktop, selecting part of the message sent by someone else on a mobile is next to impossible. You can copy all but not part, and that's where Telegram helps.

- Select part of the message in Telegram Message
- Long press on any received message, and then long press again in the message or part you want to copy. It will bring up options such as Copy and Select all.

Send High-Res Images on Telegram

Any messenger will compress the image when sent to a person or group. It saves bandwidth but also degrades quality. But if you want to send a full-size image, you can choose to send it as a file.

When sending an image of a large size, Telegram shows an option to compress the file. It can be unchecked. Another option is adding an attachment, from the gallery, choose the file to upload.

Add Sticker to Images Before Sending on Telegram

If you want to add flair, emoticons or GIFs can be used. First, select an image from the gallery, and then tap on it to make it full screen. Next, click on the edit icon, followed by the brush icon. This will open the image editor. You can select the sticker icon, choose one available, and send it.

Edit Videos Before Sending

While editing images is easy and available on messenger, Telegram tops this feature by allowing users to edit the videos. Once a video is selected, users have the options, such as cropping, trimming, or enhancing the video by changing exposure, contrast, changing RGB, etc.

Polls and Quiz Mode

Polls and Quiz mode are a great way to get an option or play games with your group. Available for groups, click on the attachment, and choose Poll. You can add questions, set up anonymous voting, allow multiple answers, or switch it to Quiz mode.

Saved Messages and Set Reminders

Telegram allows users to save messages or photos for personal use. It can be done in one of several ways.

- Click on the image and save it to the device or use the send arrow at the bottom right.

Setting a reminder is easy. Type in the message, and long press on the send button (mobile) or make a right-click on the message, and choose set reminder. Then set a time and send it.

Preview Message Without Reading

A great trick; if you want to preview a conversation without opening it, then long-press on the contact, and it will show a preview.

Create Chat Folders

Scrolling through numerous chats can be daunting. Therefore, Telegrams offers chat folders. It allows you to group a set of contacts and groups into a super folder.

Open Telegram settings, and select Folders. Users have access to personal or unread folders.

To create a new one, tap or click on the create a new folder option. Then choose to add contacts, groups, and exclude anyone you want.

Lock Chats and Application

While most phones can lock apps, Telegram offers a built-in lock feature. Go to Settings > Privacy and Security >Password Lock. Set it up, and every time it is opened, the password will be requested.

Use Multiple Accounts with Different Numbers

Unlike WhatsApp, Telegram allows users to add another Telegram accounts connected to a different number. Open Telegram settings and tap on the down arrow under your profile. Click add an account, and register with the second number.

Find People Nearby and Group

Go to Telegram Settings > Contacts and tap on Find People Nearby. You can then see people by distance, and also groups.

Slow Mode for Groups

If you maintain numerous groups, and members add messages at a rapid pace, you can slow them down. Open a group that you own, and click on the Edit icon Permissions. You can choose how long each member must wait before sending their next message. Options include between 0 to 1 min to 1 hr.

Pin Messages in a Group

If there is an important message you want everyone to see, tap on the message and then select Pin. The message will be pinned on top of the group, and when anyone taps on it, it will direct to that message.

Theme Customizer

Go to Settings > Chat Settings > and under the Color theme. Choose a predefined option, select a theme, and tap on it again. It will open the Accent Color chat; you can select a different color from the color picker. Choose between classic, day, dark, and night theme.

Chapter Ten:

Using MxM News

Cut Through the Noise

MxM News delivers curated news that cuts through the censorship, mainstream bias, and institutional dominance that has left society divided and misinformed.

The platform allows readers to access the news that matters, particularly when it is ignored. Updated minute-by-minute with news coverage from various publications and topics, readers have a one stop to be informed and stay informed.

— Donald Trump Jr. (@DonaldJTrumpJr) March 22, 2022

> The former first son, who is the epitome of reliable, fact-checked, and thorough information, told Axios: "As I travel around the country, the complaint I hear more than almost anything else is that people don't know what media outlets, journalists, or stories they can actually trust.... We created the MxM News app to help people cut through that clutter and get trustworthy news and information about topics that matter and impact their lives. We view it as an important public service and also believe it will be a great business."

What Is The MxM News App?

MxM News App topped the charts on the App Store as the latest viral app of 2022.

Along with the big names like Twitter, Instagram, and TikTok, etc., which serve as publishers, censoring anyone who disagrees with their narrative, MxM News will provide users with an unbiased information platform they can depend on as a legitimate news outlet.

As of March 2022, one of the latest smartphone apps to shine in the viral spotlight is MxM News. The app's launch was first reported by Axios on March 22. Founded in part by Donald Trump Jr., the MxM name references the app's minute-by-minute coverage for regularly updating its users on the latest stories. MxM News is an aggregation app that scours the internet for articles from other publications, so you can read them all in one place (ala Google News and Apple News).

How to use MxM News App?

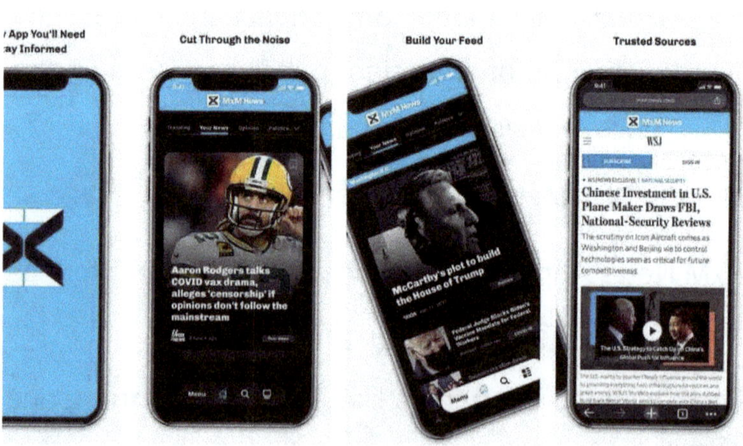

Once you have downloaded the App from either Google Play or App Store for an iPhone, you create an account directly with MxM News or sign up using your Google, Facebook, Twitter, or Apple login.

After creating an account, MxM News asks users to select topics of interest. The available categories include Politics, Policy, Life & Culture, International, Finance & Money, and America First. Then tap the blue circle (Home) in the top right corner after choosing your preferred categories. The app defaults to showing 'trending' articles, but the navigation bars allow users to filter stories by various categories. Or, search for a specific story(s)/topic, and the menu icon towards the bottom left, which has options for profile settings, display settings, etc.

Publications sources can be found from Fox News, Breitbart, New York Post, Newsmax, etc. News outlets dedicated to preserving the First Amendment (no-censorship), avoiding propaganda.

Chapter Eleven:

Using GETTR

The public version of GETTR was launched on July 4, 2021, by founder Jason Miller. The idea was to support free speech and battle against Big Tech.

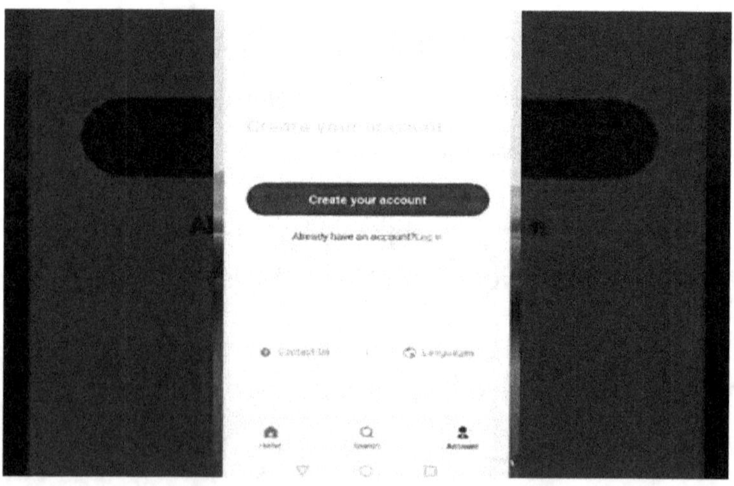

"Getter is a free speech social media site; this platform is 'cancel free,'" Miller states. "With GETTR, people will be allowed to express their thoughts and ideas freely. There will still be community guidelines and control, but that will be very limited."

The platform is user-friendly and has a beautifully designed and familiar interface.

How to use GETTR?

The platform's interface is designed around the interface of Twitter to make it easier for upcoming users to adapt and start sharing their thoughts. Plus, the platform offers a lot of functionality.

Go to GETTR.com and choose create an account option. Make sure you are connected to the internet; the platform also has Android and iOS applications.

Fill in the necessary details in the sign-up form. These details include Username, Email, and Password. You also need to accept the terms and conditions before

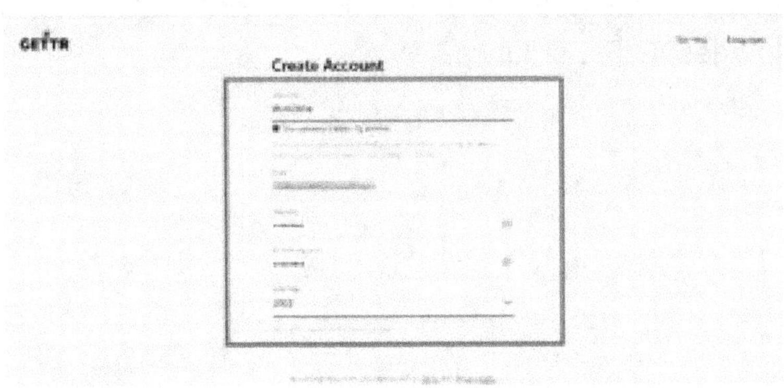

signing up; make sure you read all of them. The terms and conditions are general.

On the next page, you will be asked for the code sent to your email. Once you enter the code, your account is ready for use. Suggestions for people to follow will appear. (Following these profiles is not mandatory)

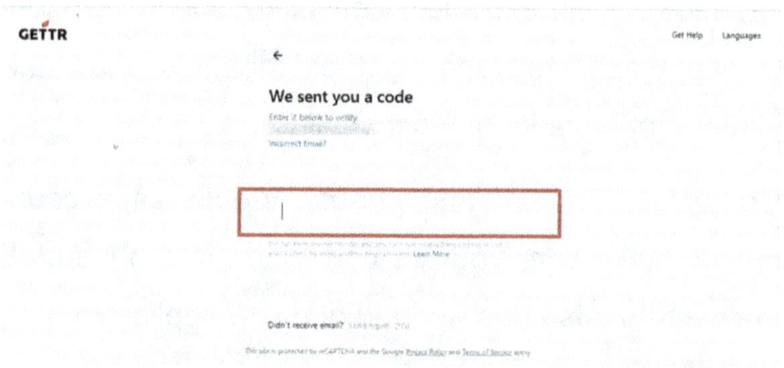

GETTR features explained

Post: The option allows users to express their opinions or make a statement. With a post, you can add Text, Images, GIFs, or Links.

Likes, Comments, Upvotes, and Reshares: On a post, you can give it a like, comment, upvote, or share.

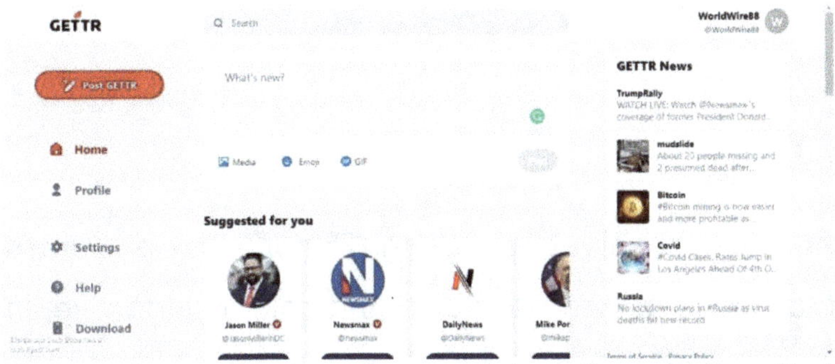

News: Getter has a news and trending section that displays news related to your interests.

Profile Section: The website has a profile section where you can upload a profile picture, add a bio, update your website, add a cover photo, and so much more. In this section, all your posts are displayed.

Conclusion

The platform works nicely, considering it has just started setting up. We also tested the Android and iOS apps for functionality, and they work fine. GETTR may add a messaging option later.

Chapter Twelve:

Using Parler

Among conservatives using Parler, the platform's promise to make free speech the norm is attractive. In July, Parler had reported 2.8 million users.

> "Speak freely and express yourself openly, without fear of being 'de-platformed' for your views," Parler states. "Engage with real people, not bots."

Some say the surge in users is not without risk. Organizations such as the Anti-Defamation League warn users that Parler's "speak freely" philosophy could lead to unsavory elements finding a place in the platform.

> State Sen. Melissa Melendez, R-Lake Elsinore, tweeted last week that she joined Parler, telling her followers: "Look forward to seeing you on @parler_app."

Parler is an American-oriented alternative media microblogging and social networking service. Like any other social media networking service, Parler is a controversial social media app that has received threats from global censorship giants on banning the app from its platform.

A Parler account would be your handle while using its services. It has a user base that mainly displays political interests. The app/website itself acts as a platform for people to share their political opinions and take on various topics.

How To Use Parler?

Parler became one of the hottest social media apps on the market in 2021. The platform prides itself on not suppressing or censoring any users' speech, regardless of their political leanings.

Steps To Post on Parler:

Start on the home screen. On the bottom right corner, click on the big blue-colored icon with a small plus/addition sign.

Once the tab opens, type your post. At the bottom of the screen, you'll notice a bar that can upload a photo, a gif, or a meme. Click on one to add as an attachment.

Commenting and Other Features:

All posts have 3 buttons to comment, echo, or upvote.

You can 'echo' a post on your home screen, which is similar to a retweet on Twitter, by clicking on the middle one.

The Upvote button is a gesture of agreement. Click on that to upvote a certain post.

How to Manage Your Parler Profile:

Click the icon on the top left of your screen with a person inside it to open a new slide menu.

Parler Profile Section

- Account Username
- Your Profile Picture
- Your Followers
- Following
- Comments
- Votes

Gear Icon

- Profile Picture
- Username
- Add Or Change a Banner
- Add Bio

Moderation Settings in Parler

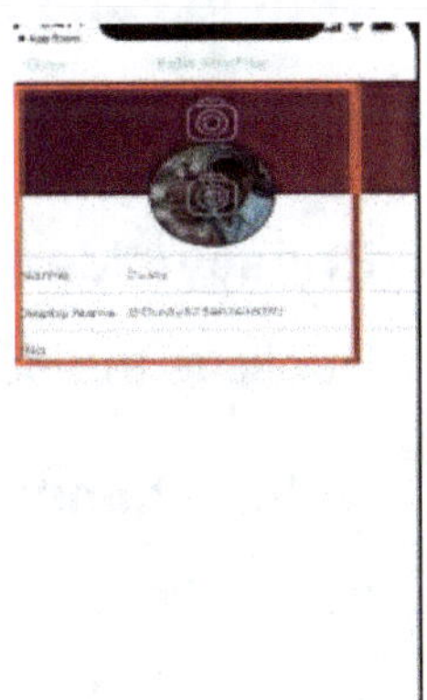

Click on the profile image; several options will open. Under this section is the Moderation feature:

- Review Comments
- Word Filters
- Settings, Etc.

Under The Comments Are Several Options:

- Review: View pending comment
- Approve: The approve button is for a pending comment.
- Mute: Mute a user or account
- Spam: Report spam users

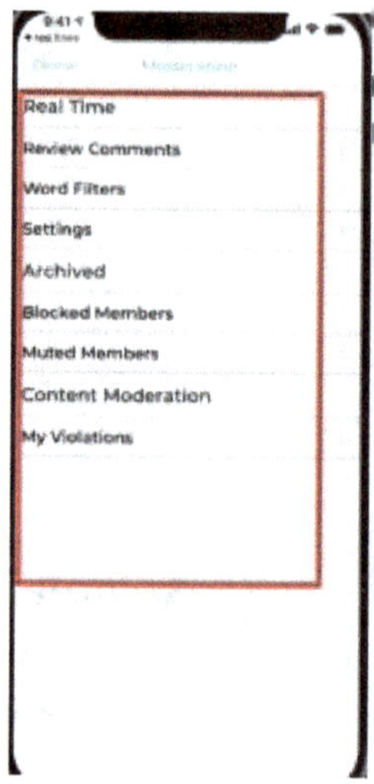

Under Settings, click on the base comment rule to make your word filter. Turn on the NSFW filter to auto-filter out NSFW comments.

Blocked members or accounts can also be seen under this section. The unblock/unmute options are in this area.

Settings and Privacy

Click on Setting and Privacy.

Privacy: Make your account private. Public is the default.

Notifications: Get emails and notifications.

Click on the Advanced filters under Settings and Privacy, to check your following, followers, and to manage which notifications you receive and from whom.

Dark mode is more appealing to some users and offers less stress on the eyes.

Discovering People and Interests

On the bottom right is the discover button, a compass icon.

- Click follow for partners and affiliates
- Click on the magnifying glass icon to search members and hashtags

Chapter Thirteen:

Using Clouthub

Clouthub is like most other social media platforms, so you can connect with other users and begin engaging.

Profile

- Add profile pic
- Cover image
- Add bio
- Add interest

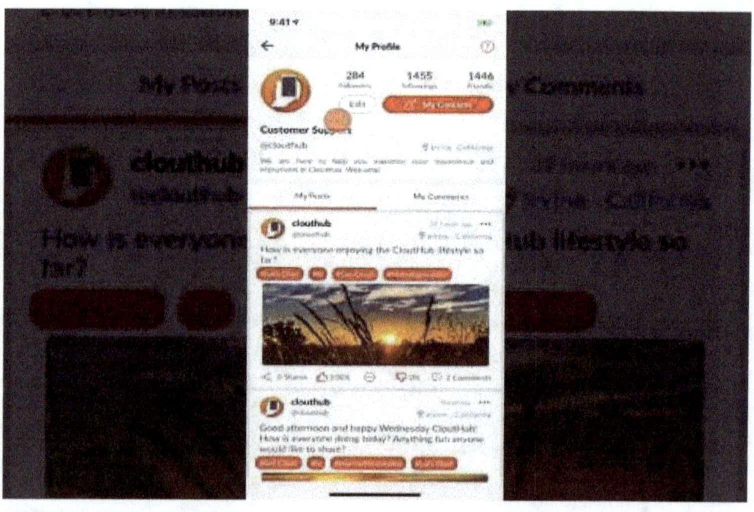

Clouthub will not share your information with third parties. The information merely helps other users learn what your interests are and connect to follow you.

At the top of the search bar, the public forum allows users to find friends. If you start typing, their name results will show, and you can tap on the avatar to see their public profile and read recent posts to decide if you want to follow or connect with them.

Invite Friends to Join

If you go to the sidebar menu and click on "My Contacts", your phone contacts will appear, you can individually invite friends. They will get a personal invitation asking them to join Clouthub.

How to Use Clouthub

On the mobile app, at the bottom is an orange tab, which opens the help overlay section. This will show what all the buttons and icons do on the current page. Just click the X in the bottom right corner to close the help overlay. If you have any questions, contact support at support@clouthub.com.

Display Username, Display Name, and Email

Users can currently update their username, email, and display name through the mobile app.

- Tap on the menu icon located at the top left to open the sidebar menu.
- Select Edit Profile under your avatar
- Tap on the Change button next to the category you want to make the changes.

After you've made the changes, tap on Save to update information.

Verify My Account

The checkmark next to the avatar is a badge, which means the account has been verified. If you want your account authenticated, it can be done through the mobile app. Below are the steps on how to verify your account.

- Tap on the menu icon located at the top left to open the sidebar menu.
- Select Settings and then choose Verification.
- Select what verification badge you want to apply for:
    - Authenticated badges are for members.

- Influencer Badge is for members who are content creators.

Users must provide valid proof they have an audience. Founder Badge is for members who have contributed to the platform and are recognized by the founder, Jeff Brain.

- You will need to submit a photo with a photo ID (driver's license, school ID, etc.).
- Review the Request Verification and make the necessary changes if needed.
- Tap on Submit when you are done.

This is just an option and not mandatory.

Change Notifications

- Go to Groups
- Tap on your avatar located on the right, then select Account Settings
- Select Email & Notifications then toggle on the switch next to Receive email notifications

How to Change or Reset Passwords

Password changes can be made by going to Settings and selecting update password. You will need to provide your current password, enter your new password, and verify it.

Passwords can also be reset from the home screen under the sign-in option. You will need to choose which method to receive a verification code (text message for mobile phone or phone call for landline phone).

Clouthub users are not censored unless the content is inappropriate, such as pron. But sometimes the AI cannot tell what is in an image, so it's sent to the staff for review. Generally, this review process only results in a momentary delay, and once the post is approved, it will be published. Posts that violate the Terms of Use will be rejected, and members are welcome to contact support@clouthub.com if they feel they did not violate the terms.

Clouthub does not and will never engage in censorship of ideas and issues. We encourage robust discussion of ideas and issues from all sides.

Clouthub Posts in Forum

- Go to Settings (located on the sidebar menu for mobile app, located at the left window on the website).
- Choose Public Post Visibility.
- Choose View all members' posts and tap on Save. You can change this back anytime.
- If a member is inactive for the next 15 days, it will set it back to view only followers' posts.

For new members, all posts will automatically be visible for 30 days. Afterward, it will be set to view only followers. The feature can be modified in Settings.

Editing a Post

- Simply tap on your post's option (...) on the top right to open options and select Edit this post.

Like Posts

- Tap the lightbulb and it will turn orange indicating you have liked the post.

Creating a New Group

To create a group, we suggest using the website version on a desktop. Here is the link to the website: https://app.clouthub.com/login.

- Tap on the Groups tab located at the top.
- Click on the + icon next to your avatar on the right and select Group.
- Fill in your group's information. The color section is the background color for your banner (do not enter color code).
- Tap on Create button when you are done.

Group Administrators can modify the header image.

- Tap on the options icon (...) next to the moderate button.
- Select to upload an image for icon and banner.

Sharing With Non-Members

- Tap on the Groups tab located at the top.
- Tap on the group's thumbnail to open their page.
- On the right side below the group banner, there is a Share Group window. Tap where you want

to share your group: LinkedIn, Facebook, Twitter, WhatsApp, or email.

- Non-members can view all the posts on the group's page, but they cannot interact with members such as like or comment without a Clouthub account.

Delete Group

- To delete your group, tap on the options icon (...) next to the Moderate button on the header and select Delete Group.

Chapter Fourteen:

SEO Optimization: It's all about the algorithms

Search Engine Optimization (SEO) is the process of improving a website or app's presence in organic (free) search results. SEO differs from paid search campaigns where a marketer must pay for placement in search results.

What is an SEO Audit?

An SEO audit is a review of a website, with the intent of improving the site's rankings in organic search results. The assessments are performed with specialized tools, or by an experienced SEO consultant.

Why Audit a website or App?

There are several reasons to consider an audit, but the most common are:

a) Organic traffic has declined
b) A redesign of a website or app

c) Site migration

d) Consolidation

e) Rebrand

f) Or other major technical, content, link-related events

Technical debate (refactoring is not only a result of poorly written code but is also done based on an evolving understanding of a problem, and the best way to solve that problem) has been built upon your website. Several items can cause this issue to escalate; for example, plugins or other technology can interfere with functionality, or worse yet, get in the way of search engine bots, browsers, and users.

Website content must stay updated to keep your site ranking high in search engine results, along with eliminating outdated keywords.

- If the website contains content duplication it may cause an over indexation or eroding of page authority. The issue lowers search engine results.
- Any blocked or hidden content could cause indexation concerns. Users will be restricted

from finding your website if search engines cannot find all the present content.

- If your website has slower load times, visitors find the issue frustrating and it signals search engines to assign a lower rank. It will lower organic SEO results and conversion rates.
- A website that is not secure (HTTPS) could risk your visitors' privacy and can trigger warnings in their browser. It is becoming increasingly important to have a more secure site. The same concept applies to sites that are non-transactional, especially if competitors have HTTPS security protocols.
- Poor mobile sites can lead to unsatisfied visitors, climbing bounce rate, and decreased keyword rankings based on Google's understanding of low user satisfaction.
- Broken links (links from your website to other websites), inbound links (links from other websites to yours), or internal links (links from one page of your site to another) may lower your site's trust and authority.

- Google Webmaster Guidelines not being followed may lead to the devaluation of the site, making it less visible to users.

SEO Audits

The best practices for an audit are once or twice a year; however, it can vary depending on the industry or content strategy. Some examples:

- Website content changes regularly
- Code changes frequently on your website
- Multiple individuals contribute to your site
- Your industry changes quickly online
- Your industry is highly competitive online

The best way to think of having an SEO audit is by getting an annual physical with your doctor, or a wellness exam. Results show potential problems on the existing site, solutions to solve the issues, along with recommendations to increase performance.

Benefits of an SEO Audit

- Identify technical problems to resolve site performance in search engine results, thereby improving organic searches.
- Identify content opportunities

- Digital health analytics
- Current backlink profile
- Improve the overall use of the website for users and search engines
- Elevate rankings related to keyword searches, increase conversations through leads and online sales.
- Establish a passive income through marketing channels
- Learn how search engines are viewing the website

What SEO Audits Include

Performance audits can include the following depending on your situation:

- Domains
- Subdomains
- URLs
- Redirects
- 404 page
- Robots.txt
- Indexing issues
- Crawl issues
- Canonicalization issues

- Page load time
- Structured data recommendations
- HTML and XML sitemaps
- Navigation and file structure
- Template-specific recommendations
- Internal linking strategies
- External linking strategies
- Keywords
- Page titles and meta tags
- Content
- Duplicate content
- Thin pages
- Under-optimized pages
- Data feed optimization
- Conversions
- Analytics
- Webmaster accounts
- Local targeting
- Citation improvements
- Image optimization
- Mobile optimization
- International targeting
- Google News inclusion

- Digital assets
- Social media indicators
- Blog optimization
- Information architecture
- Usability concerns
- Coordination with ADA requirements
- Knowledge graph optimization

How are SEO Audits Received?

Once the initial audit is completed, the analytics will be evaluated by one of our experts and then a meeting will be planned to review the results. A strategy can be created to solve the issues.

Free SEO Audit Tools

- **Google Search Console** is consulted before any actions. The domains must be accepted.
- **Google Analytics** – Analytics are crucial to the SEO audit process. Data provides the ability to track Key Performance Indicators (KPIs) and measure the impact of the recommendations for the audit results. The data provided in Google Analytics allows us to track specific KPIs and measure the impact of the recommendations contained in the SEO audit deliverables.

- **Bing Webmaster Tools** – Bing Webmaster Tools provide insights that are not contained in any of the Google tools.
- **Chrome Developer Tools** – These tools allow the user to see how crawlers and browsers interact with your site. The page speed is crucial to any SEO audit. Chrome Developer Tools reveal which page elements are slowing users down.

Paid SEO Audit Tools

The paid tools for an SEO audit are almost endless, but below are a few of the favorites.

- MOZ – Keyword Research
- STAT – Keyword Rank Tracking
- PitchBox – Outreach Prospecting, Campaign Management, and Reporting
- Spyfu – Keyword Research and Competitive Analysis
- Ahrefs – Backlink Analysis, Outreach Prospecting, and Competitive Analysis
- Content King – Content Performance Tracking and Monitoring
- Crawlers

- Screaming Frog – Website Crawling and Searching and Extracting Code
- Deep Crawl – Web-based Crawling of Large Websites

Arguments for and Against SEO Audit Tools

SEO audit tools can eat up a budget with little to no results, or the user finds the analytics vague and complicated, so it's important to understand your current needs. Granted, the tools give wonderful tracking performance if you don't have a robust team to sort through the particulars; however, the cost may be a wasteful resource. The best results come from a well-planned strategy, and that comes from individuals. In some cases, the financial expense may bring forth unexpected results in the end.

International SEO Marketing

Glossary definitions: "Hreflang tags are a technical solution for sites that have similar content in multiple languages. The owner of a multilingual site wants search engines to send people to the content in their language. Say a user is Dutch and the page that ranks is English, but there's also a Dutch version."

Domain names for international SEO. You may want to consider a few things when choosing a domain name for your international SEO campaigns. Some domains, known as country code top-level domains (ccTLD), will default to a specific location.

Website Expansion

The aspects of international SEO are wildly misunderstood. The intricacies are more than HREFLANG, ccTLDs (country-targeted top-level domains), and geo-targeting. It's imperative to map the expansion campaign and understand the market in the areas you want to expand into.

If you have decided to increase your brand internationally, there are several items to learn before changing the site settings. Items of interest:

- The countries into which you're expanding
- Those countries' main languages, and
- How your business offerings might change in the new markets

Writer's Publishing House Social Media Marketing has the tools to offer such expansion in the event your company wants to grow its brand internationally.

Languages

Business offerings across the web must incorporate different languages, to accommodate translating content so search engines can guide users to the best options.

Action Items:

- Translations are best done manually; it is the best option for branding issues and user preferences.
- Put your HREFLANG in XML sitemaps. However, this is not your only option, except that it keeps code off your page. This will increase page speed.
- Don't use a ccTLD. It is for Geo-targeting only.

Keep in Mind:

It is not necessary to change the ccTLDs or geotargeting; producing good translations and using the correct site markup will get the desired results.

SEO Marketing for Local Branding

In many businesses, there is one common struggle that is difficult to avoid: competitors. The goal must be to gain traction over other local retailers. Although, going against the larger companies with auto-generated local listings is challenging. Plus, years of playing the SEO game increases the difficulty.

One of the most demanding obstacles for many local businesses is how to stay up to date with Google's ever-evolving list of ranking factors; updates like the "Possum" can disrupt any strategy. The algorithm changes allowed businesses outside city limits to compete for local spots if they service that area.

Ten SEO Tips to Help Move the Needle for Local Market Branding

Claim Your Business Listings

Once you have claimed your business listing, it is time to claim any duplicate listings that develop over time. The listings can be claimed and then any duplicates can be removed. Finding the listings can seem daunting, but there are tools to assist in this process. Moz Local is one great option to locate all local listings.

The process is easy: First, enter the business name and zip code. Be specific on the business spelling, capitalizations, abbreviations, etc. Select your business from the results and Moz will serve you the complete, incomplete, inconsistent, and duplicate listings tied to your business.

Add Location Pages to Your Website

To get the best results when search engines crawl your site for the best possible matches, it is important to have a specific landing page for each of your business locations. The address should include suite numbers and the exact physical location.

Improve NAP Consistency

What is NAP?

"The acronym NAP stands for Name, Address, Phone number, and it's critical for any business that wants to rank well in local organic search results" (Corona, 2018).

Search engines need to have accurate information on the business name, address, and phone number (NAP), and this information must be consistent everywhere.

The information must be specific, not just your name and address. For example, if the title includes LLC, Co., or Inc., add the acronyms. Be consistent with the information listed on the website.

The Moz local search tool allows much of the information to be updated. Start with the Google Business Listing.

Update Everything on my Google My Business

Accurate information is imperative for everyday traffic across the Internet, particularly for optimized SEO search engine results.

Log into your Google My Business (GMB) account and update any outdated information. It is very important to fill in as much information as possible. Be thorough.

The listing should be appealing:

- Logo
- Avatar/profile pic
- Interior photos
- Exterior photos
- Product photos

All images should be high-quality resolutions. You only get one chance at a first impression. Update the info for all business locations.

Attain Reviews

One of the most important factors in allowing your business to grow is reviews. People want to read what others have thought of your services, products, or customer service. Good reviews pack a powerful punch; however, the reviews must be legitimate, so do not fake them. If customers receive quality service, writing a review will not be a problem.

The reviews not only help your business ranking, but they also increase search results. By expanding real estate on a web search, SEO results will improve. As your demand increases, so will your Google ranking.

Peer ranking is a highly social advantage. When users see a 5-star review it tackles three major components at one time:

- Ranking
- Click-through rate (CTR)
- Conversion rate optimization (CRO)

Create Local Content

When you create content in the business niche it will make an impact on the local search ranking.

Google AdWords Keyword Planner

AdWords Keyword Planner is a great FREE tool when it comes to establishing your local SEO keywords. The research will offer keywords that have the highest search volume along with the lowest. Plus, it helps you find similar terms for local audiences.

Backlinks from Partners and Sponsorships

Create a list of businesses and organizations that you partner with or sponsor, and then contact them and ask that they add a link to their website. Make sure you reciprocate the offer.

Local Link Building

Gaining backlinks from high-domain authority websites will highly impact your local presence. This is one area that cannot be stressed enough.

Utilize Social Media Platforms

Do not underestimate the usage of social media platforms. They are a powerful financial asset at your fingertips. Plus, it's free marketing. Google will crawl and pull search results from social platforms, such as Facebook profiles and reviews, your business's LinkedIn or YouTube, and even Twitter accounts and recent tweets.

In the next section are some suggestions on optimizing for local SEO growth. According to SEO Expert, "The ways of how we search using search engines and the content delivered to us are always changing. But one thing for sure is that search engines are clearly on a mission to provide users with the most relevant results for their query, personalized based on their location, search history, and browsing behavior" (Shaw, 2019).

The following is a checklist you can follow to optimize to grow a local business:

- Boost SEO by adding keywords to any website
- Include business contact information such as name, address, and phone number (NAP).
- Always encourage customers to leave quality reviews. If you need to remove a Facebook review, read this.
- Be prompt when responding to reviews, even if it is negative. You will not be able to please everyone all the time, but use the knowledge to better your customer service.
- Upload at least ten quality photographs so users will recognize your business quickly.
- Stay active. Keep business profiles updated with the latest news.

Chapter Fifteen:

Reputation Management

What is Reputation Management?

It is one of the most important factors of owning or operating a business. Negative reviews or reputations can be difficult to overcome unless the situation is handled correctly. Negative events that can impact reputation in a single instant may include scandals, criminal acts, product recalls, bad press, lawsuits, negative reviews, etc.

Online Reputation Management (ORM)

Since the development of the Internet, companies have emerged all over to manage reputation issues. Search results like Google, social media sites, Yelp, and beyond can surface after a negative incident.

Five Ways to Get Started with Reputation Marketing

1) **Audit content:** One of the first steps to controlling online reputation is actively participating in content inventories. Address all concerns about the online content before releasing it to any public site. Head off all feedback from followers or editorials about you or your business.

2) **Track conversations:** The adage "You only get one shot at a first impression" rings true. Once the public experiences an organization, business, company, or person, a reputation is formed. It can be good, bad, or anything in between.

Track all conversations to measure quality sentiment. Then, learn areas of opportunity to improve your brand. Always maintain control of the content, conversation, and communication among stakeholders.

3) **Install reputation marketers:** Every business needs management, especially in the area of reputation. It is best to either hire someone or maintain a high level of scrutiny over the content

being released. The action will help control the company's mission statement.

4) **Coaching consistency:** Any successful business runs on consistency; it is a necessary evil to ensure a quality reputation among the public. Anyone involved, no matter how small a part they play, should know and understand their role in your mission brand.

5) **Empowering surprise:** One unexpected marketing advantage is the element of surprise. It can be categorized as the moment when a customer is amazed by your company and becomes ready to spread the good word. However, surprise cannot be a normal event. Instead, use the quality of work produced to motivate customers to enhance your brand organically.

Videos

Video marketing has been on a steady rise for years. In fact, according to Forrester Research[1] videos show 50% more organic first-page searches than traditional text pages. I'd say that is an impressive beginning!

One main reason for creating online marketing videos is they are an attractive way to connect with potential clients. Plus, video production is relatively inexpensive. Once the recording is finished, it can stay online forever. In other words, the benefits outweigh the cost of marketing over time.

In addition to the online benefits, video marketing and social media go hand in hand since most social media platforms encourage posting and sharing to promote engagement. The opportunities to have a video go viral are limitless. Let's get recording!

If this is your first time creating a video, we have some suggestions to help make it a success:

1) **Title:** Like with any marketing plan, the title is highly important. It is what will bring impressions and encourage people to share and repost. Don't forget the appropriate keywords in your title. They will help online search engines to locate your channel, website, or social media profile.
2) **Content:** It's important to write good content. The same applies to any marketing venue: content, content, and better content. Tip: Keep

all videos short until you have a faithful following. At that point, you can study analytics.

3) **A good length is between 3 to 5 mins. URL:** One way to engage the audience is to use the add text box to your video. It's a great tool for adding a website address, tips, special messages, sales, or requests.
4) **Branding Images:** During the video, it's important to display your business logo. You can keep it as a permanent image or flash it several times during the process. The best possible place to display the brand is the upper left-hand corner.
5) **HTML Link:** A common mistake is leaving out the hyperlink to direct traffic. If viewers like your information, they will want to locate you easily. One way to deter traffic is by not making yourself available to be contacted by potential clients.
6) **Video Reach:** Many marketers limit themselves to YouTube, however, video marketing goes beyond the average video channels. Websites are the best way to connect with internet traffic, so why not captivate them on your website or app?

Finally, Google algorithms factor impressions into any organic search results. Embedded video views receive a much higher rating for search analytics.

Reasons Any Company Needs Video Marketing

Wonder why you should be using video marketing? Honestly stated, "YouTube is the 2nd largest search engine on the web and by 2020, 75% of mobile traffic will be video," according to Cisco (Buffa, 2013).

In other words, if your business does not yet video market, it is time to start. Video marketing provides the following advantages:

1) **Increases engagement:** Statistics prove time again that visual content is key to user engagement. One of the main reasons is the ease of shareability across social media. Think back to the reason social media was created: to socialize. What better way to engage with an audience than a video? "Audiences are about 10 times more likely to engage, share, and comment on video content compared to blogs

or related social posts. In fact, videos on Facebook business pages increase end-user engagement by 33%. Take our Starbucks Unicorn Frapp video as an example! This was a fun video our team made together trying out current trends and got 1.4k views on Facebook" (Readyartwork, n.d.).

2) **Add personality to your brand:**
Yes, pictures are said to be worth a thousand words, but videos can bring millions to your brand.

According to readyartwork, "Videos are perfect for company branding and increase brand awareness by 52%." This alone is a very good reason to start a video marketing strategy.

3) **Showcase your products or services:** One question, why use a flat image when you can create a 3D realm to cabinet and display the usage of a product? For example, why display a pair of shoes when you can highlight the color and see the product in use?
4) **Provide visual explanations:** "The human brain prefers visuals, in fact, 90% of information

transmitted to the brain is visual and people retain 80% of what they see in comparison to only 20% of what they read! So, don't make it difficult for your customers. Instead make it visual, like this informative conservation video we made for the City of Monrovia. A large amount of text would be so exhausting to read, but as a video, the information is more easily retained and understood" (readyartwork, n.d.).

5) **Show your company's accomplishments:** It is important to showcase achievements and capabilities to current followers or potential clients. Videos are a perfect way to capture users' attention.
6) **Elevate retention rates on your website**: "If the content is in a video, 65% of viewers watch more than ¾ of a video, which is more than most text-based content. Videos on retail sites keep visitors an average of 2 minutes longer so your company can capitalize on this by utilizing a video loop on your website" (readyartwork, n.d.).

A video is the first and last thing visitors see on your website, so why not entice them to stay longer and review all the services offered?

7) **Increase conversion rates and boost sales:** The main reason to use video marketing is to improve customer sales. "Studies also show that 85% of customers are more likely to purchase after watching a product video" (readyartwork, n.d.).

Podcasts

Ever since our ancestors started drawing or carving on cave walls, the importance of storytelling has played a crucial role in the advancement of society. The ancient scrolls of humans are revered; a cherished heritage that we can learn about the past. And this is a concept that continues to radiate among current generations.

Video has somewhat diminished the allure of using podcasts in some areas of entertainment, but they have flourished in many avenues since the invention of smart mobile technology. Podcasts can be created to directly communicate with the listener. It is a more intimate way of passing the information along to the subscriber.

A valuable asset of podcasts is they are an easy, convenient way to communicate. They can be downloaded on any digital device and taken anywhere, unlike videos that require more memory and connection to watch.

Creating podcasts can deliver a digital marketing outlet that reduces the costs associated with postage, printing, or paper-generated products. Plus, they are compatible with email restrictions on file size.

Because podcasts are delivered digitally, they eliminate many costs associated with other forms of communication. They can also reduce meeting costs and e-mail storage costs. They are easy to archive and updating them is quick and easy.

In society, time efficiency is highly important to many business owners, and using podcasts for clients is an effective use of their time. It's something they can consume while meeting the daily demands of life. By saving time, you can improve productivity.

One last suggestion: Podcasts are a great way to develop your social networking strategy. Over time, subscribers are essential to deepening the effectiveness of your brand.

Why Blog, Blog, and More Blogging?

The benefits of blogging are limitless for any business. If you think for a moment about how many times you were unsure of how something is done, the first thing you did was Google search the topic. What happens? You get results on the subject matter. At that point, you can determine the best site to find answers. The majority of listings are blogs of some kind. Blogging has become the new age of encyclopedias. Below are the advantages of blogging:

1. Drives website traffic
2. Helps turn traffic into leads
3. Creates the authority status of the author
4. Brings forth long-term results
5. Provides opportunities for guest blogging

Blog posts provide consistent traffic each day. Many of these potential leads will come from blog articles, although it's important to incorporate all the marketing tools we have discussed in the various sections of this book.

One additional option for blogging is to test large campaigns at minimal costs. By building an audience for the new product or whatever the campaign may be, you can save money using property that's already owned. Instead of investing in advertising with someone else, get some response from current followers. After the results are analyzed it will be easier to make any necessary adjustments before publishing a big campaign.

Any company or small business can benefit from a blog. It has also become popular with individuals who want to tell their stories or educate the public on certain topics. Happy blogging!

The Best Blogging Tools & Resources

- Mindmeister
- Evernote
- Trello
- Google Calendar
- Focus Booster
- Unroll.me
- Sidekick.com
- Dropbox.com

- Statscount
- Screenflow
- Pdf Escape
- Grammerly.com
- Blogger.com
- Transcribe
- Google alerts.com
- Wisestamp
- shareaholic.com
- Triberr:
- Scoop.it
- Pocket

Webinars

One of the best marketing solutions is using a cross-platform. Since the invention of the Internet, the medium of marketing outlets has expanded dramatically. One such option is offering webinars for current clients or potential clients. It is a highly effective way to sell products and services.

Webinar marketing is one way to connect with a broader audience and promote your business. Most webinar tools provide free lead generation options and offer essential information on improving ROI at the end of the webinar.

A normal webinar presentation consists of the presenter's program, followed by a Q&A session. Due to the visual medium, it is much easier to connect with participants since most people are visual learners. Some webinar presentation ideas include:

- Expound on products or services or sometimes both
- Educate on published content or blog postings
- Lecture on a particular service

One word of caution: Webinars are not a sales pitch. You must provide the participants with a valuable service to improve their life. By educating them on your product or service, it grants them the opportunity to make a purchase.

According to MakeSocialMediaSell, webinars retain 40% of the viewers' attention. Up to that 40% who attend will become qualified leads. The additional percentage will buy something from your services. However, only half of the registered individuals will attend the webinar. But the results seen by other companies endeavor a worthwhile risk.

There is one key point that any marketing tool must include: Make sure you offer a solution to ease the participant's pain. Then provide options for solving the issues with outlets. Always let the customer decide the best choice that suits their needs.

The ideal period is 60 minutes, shutting down in 45 minutes and opening the floor to questions. Or, another option would be to take a ten-minute break after 30 minutes for communication with participants, then end with another option for additional questions. It's critical to be highly organized and prepared. You are the expert! Below are some webinar hosting services:

- GotoWebinar
- Cisco WebEx
- ClickMeeting
- Anymeeting
- Instant Teleseminar
- Zoom
- WebinarJam
- EasyWebinar

If you are concerned about financial restraints, YouTube Live is a free option and wildly popular. The video can be made available on Wistia or Vimeo.

Chapter Sixteen:

Running Ads

In literal terms, advertising is the process of making your business merchandise or services known to an audience. It is generally done through some type of media outlet. It's a creative positioning in the media, in a timely fashion, used in a specific strategic way.

The best uses of advertising money involve designing a campaign that aligns with the wants and needs of your client's genre. The key is to generate excitement for a product or service. These questions are very important when designing an advertising campaign:

- Who are you?
- Why should someone do business with your company?
- What will they get from your product or services?

There are some major differences between marketing and advertising that you should be aware of and understand. Firstly, marketing is the concept of preparing a product for the marketplace. Secondly, advertising is the act of placing the product before an audience. If you find the difference between the two confusing, you are not alone.

Advertising is only one segment of the marketing process. The ability to run an ad is done by purchasing the ad space. It's an announcement that is created by an identifiable sponsor, brand, or business logo to persuade an audience to buy the product. The advertisement placement can be anywhere, like magazines, direct mail, email, websites, blogs, TV, radio, or public transit.

Marketing, on the other hand, is the methodical preparation and application of controlling the mix between intended buyers and sellers for the beneficial exchange of products and services. Marketing is a step-by-step process that starts with selling your merchandise – a short compelling description to explain your business. Think of marketing as one piece of the pie. The rest includes advertising, market research, media planning, community relations, and sales strategy. Intermingled with all this is customer service, a huge portion of any successful business. The preparation of any advertising campaign is critical to its success.

Reasons to Consider Paid Social Media Advertising

According to The State of Tech, "92% of small businesses will increase their investment in social media this year." (Heing, 2018).

If you are still wondering why you should pay for social media advertising, keep reading. Statistics prove that more than two billion users are on social media each day. It breaks down to 135 minutes in 24 hours.

One tip: Paid social media advertising is quite different than traditional outbound marketing. Since the initiation of Big Data, the ability to pinpoint exact target audiences is simple. Social media platforms are designed to facilitate the achievement of business goals such as lead generation, website traffic, brand awareness, and much more. Ad programs also grant access to native analytics to help improve campaign success.

Below are seven advantages of using paid social media advertising:

- Amplify your reach
- Fit any budget
- Enhance your targeting
- Boost brand awareness
- Maximize your content marketing
- Gain access to mobile users
- Gather market insights

1) **Amplify Reach:** Marketing helps to promote brand visibility. Since the sheer volume of posts has increased exponentially, the statistical chance of people seeing your posts has declined significantly. In the case of paid ads campaigns, they are guaranteed to be placed on a user's feed. Despite the noise of the larger social platform, this gives you a direct window to drive leads, website traffic, and sales. Success will come when you find where your audience spends their time online.

2) **Fit Any Budget:** Paid marketing is a highly cost-effective way to promote businesses. The ads are run on a pay-per-click (PPC) schedule. This means

you pay when someone clicks on the link, plus you get the benefit of impressions. In other words, free advertising. One advantage is the ability to advertise with your niche markets at a discount. Once a few ad cycles have run, you can refine the targeting to drive better ROI.

3) **Enhance Targeting:** Paid advertising lets the user have complete control over the ad and their audience. All the platforms allow for a plethora of targeting parameters. Factors include interests, hobbies, personality types, and more. By uploading a list of contacts to target, or creating a similar audience, gives a powerful base for expanding to an ideal audience.
4) **Boost Brand Awareness:** The social media campaign is the most cost-effective way to expand your brand reach. When your business appears in the regular News Feed users will recognize and begin to engage with posts.

> "Consider that 80% of its users follow at least one brand on Instagram. Of this majority group, at least 30% of users have purchased a

product they discovered on Instagram" (Heing, 2018).

5) **Maximize Content Marketing:** Social media is one of the best ways to circulate brand awareness.

> "According to Sprout Social, 73.4% of users follow a brand because they're interested in its product or service. Nurture the curiosity of your followers with educational content that will transform them into qualified leads" (Heing, 2018).

This will not only increase social media traffic, but will also drive website traffic, boost engagement on social media, and improve the ROI of your content marketing.

6) **Access Mobile Users Anytime:** The penetration of social media advertising is unparalleled. "According to Pew Research, 80% of the time spent on social media is spent on a mobile device" (Heing, 2018).

When businesses pay for social media advertising, users will see the ads and learn about how to purchase the products. The most effective ads emulate the organic content of their native platform.

7) **Gather Market Insights:** Several questions can be answered with social media, such as:
    1. How did your audience interact with your ads?
    2. Which ad type was most popular?
    3. Did video convert better – and with whom?

The use of native analytics on social media platforms helps to assess and refine the performance of advertising campaigns. Look to KPIs such as clicks, comments, and profile visits to determine if your ads are creating an impact.

All the social media platforms indeed have their brand of advertising, however, that does not mean business owners should use each one of them. The first step is to study which one performs organically the best. In other words, find the best possible fit for your product or services.

Once you have decided which outlet is the best option for your business it's time to look at the types of ads that are available.

GAB Ads

GAB designed its ads to help achieve one of three types of campaign intentions:

- Awareness
- Consideration
- Conversion

Awareness: This is the act of building an audience that knows or follows your company. Branding is the essence of running a successful business.

Consideration: Using the consideration objective will drive traffic to your website, increase engagement, encourage app installs, or improve video views. Plus, the ad can generate leads and encourage communication.

Conversion: The basic use of conversions is to improve online conversations and drive traffic to an offline store.

GAB is becoming a popular demographic that has the potential for driving enormous brand awareness if used in the right fashion.

Several Formats Are Available:

Photo Ads

When you run a GAB ad it includes a photo and 125 characters of text. The text incorporates the title and link description, plus call-to-action buttons. The option also applies to posts that can be promoted.

Video Ads

Video ads can also work well with a TV ad campaign. The TV part of the ad does not have to align with the same content, because it is a great way to draw in an audience. It can be used to highlight the best part of your brand.

Tip: The best results will come from videos that are 15 seconds or less.

Carousel Ads

A unique adoption is carousel advertising. They allow business owners to create ads with up to 10 images or videos. Each one includes an individual link. One particular option with this type of marketing is having the ability to showcase different features of a product or service or explain a process for multiple products.

Tip: When creating an ad, it must provide a story. Lead the follower in, tell the story, and solve their problem.

Slideshow Ads

These types of ads create a video using static images. It offers compelling motion, yet requires no video resources. It's a great alternative to video ads.

Tip: Slideshow ads load quickly, even at slower connection speeds.

Collection Ads

These ads are a great way to show products right in the profile feed. They include a cover photo or video. You can add product images with pricing along with other details. Users can learn more about your business.

Tip: These are perfect for travel agencies or other destination offers.

Lead Ads

Lead ads are only on mobile devices and include pre-populated contact forms. They are a great way to build an email database or get users to sign up for a newsletter, request a free trial, or quote. The leads can create a good sales funnel.

Tip: For the best results, collect the most information upfront as possible.

LinkedIn Ads

LinkedIn is the world's largest business stage. It makes sense to target goods dollar to dollar. The following steps will have you mastering LinkedIn like a breeze.

Objectives:

- Build brand awareness
- Drive website traffic
- Generate leads and convert prospects

Audience considerations: Business owners have rated LinkedIn as the best platform for B2B lead generation. LinkedIn is a professional networking platform. It offers targeting options based on professional qualifications like job title and seniority.

LinkedIn Ad Types

- Sponsored Content
- Sponsored InMail
- Text Ads

Sponsored Content

These ads will show in the news feed on mobile and desktop devices. The results expose content to a larger audience and give you the ability to showcase your brand.

Tip: Keep headlines under 150 characters, and use larger images to gain higher click-through rates. The recommended sizes are 1200 x 627 pixels.

According to Hootsuite, “The customer service software company Aspect used Sponsored Content to promote its thought leadership articles. The campaign increased Company Page followers by 17 percent and referral traffic to the Aspect blog by four times.” (Hootsuite, n.d.)

Sponsored InMail

If you chose a sponsored mail option, the user can reach beyond the clients’ news feed. The ads are sent through the inbox, and it’s one way to deliver personalized messages. You can also use call-to-action buttons.

Ads Reach

- Attract more leads
- Have more and better conversations
- Send personalized invites to webinars and other events
- Target promotions to the right audience
- Promote content like downloadable eBooks and white papers

Tip: The best results come when body text is under 500 characters. The top five performing calls-to-action for Sponsored InMail are: Try, Free, Today, Click, and Apply.

Text Ads

These campaigns are a wonderful way to drive traffic to your LinkedIn Company page or website. They are similar to Google or Bing search ads.

For any business, it's best to create variations of the same ad. For example, clone the ad and then change the headline, slightly. Once the ad runs for some time, it will show the results and grant the ability to refine the specs. However, these ads only run on desktops, so it is a great way to attract busy professionals to glance at the news feed.

Ads Reach

- Fast and easy to get started
- Set your budget
- Choose your audience with laser-sharp B2B filters
- Track conversions
- Choose your model: cost-per-click or cost-per-thousand-impressions

Despite the name, text ads can include a thumbnail image of 50 x 50 pixels.

Tip: Use a human face such as a profile image for the best results.

Business Objectives:

- Collect leads
- Drive website traffic
- Build brand awareness and extend your reach
- Increase product and brand consideration
- Attract new viewers

- Grow your subscriber base

Audience considerations:

According to HubSpot, "YouTube is the only social network used by more men than women. The difference is not huge: 75 percent of American men use YouTube, and 72 percent of American women. But this may be of interest if you're specifically targeting a male audience." (Hubspot, n.d.)

Chapter Seventeen:

Graphic Design

The Vark Model shows us that the human brain is 90% visual.

"It is estimated that 40% of people prefer visual learning over auditory or kinaesthetic," Neil Fleming.

Therefore, graphic design is more than just pictures, graphs, or drawings. It is a crucial form of communication and problem solving for most humans. In the business world, it's an effective element to use to engage with consumers.

Graphic design is essential to building brand awareness, which in turn influences the customer's decision-making process. Below are some elements involved in quality graphic design:

1. Call to action (CTA): Persuading an action
2. Infographic: Sparks an interest
3. Blog post graphics: Visual content

Essentially, graphic design is an appealing way for companies to interact with their audience, hence the reason for social media's success. Design elements within content marketing will help sway prospects to learn more about your product, funneling conversation.

In conclusion, humans are visual creatures; when the brain stores detail it's done in two ways, verbal and visual. But when considering these factors in your marketing plan, consider that people don't recall decorative or arbitrary images, so you must illustrate something memorable to the person. This means the message will be committed to memory.

Affordable Graphic Design Tools

- Canva: Creative Platform for Graphic Designers
- Pic Monkey: Photo Editing and Design Website
- Inkscape: A powerful vector graphics tool that's free and open-source
- Krita: Free software packed with advanced drawing aids and templates
- GIMP: An incredible tool for any designer who works with photos
- Blender: The ultimate free tool for graphic designers creating 3D content

- Easel.ly: Online web tool to create visual infographics
- Adobe Graphic Programs
    - Photoshop
    - Illustrator
    - InDesign
    - XD
    - Lightroom
    - Premier Rush
    - Fresco
    - Audition
    - Character Animator
    - InCopy
    - Dreamweaver
    - Dimension
    - 3D designers
- Envato
    - Stock Video
    - Video Templates
    - Music
    - Sound Effects
    - Graphic Templates
    - Graphics
    - Presentation Templates

    - Photos
    - Fonts
    - Web Templates
- Elementor – WordPress Website Add-on Program
- Placeit
- Smartmock-ups

Chapter Eighteen:

Grants & Loans for Entrepreneurs

"The amount of new business being launched in the United States grows dramatically. According to the US Small Business Administration (US Small Business Administration, n.d.) (SBA), in 2010 there were 27.9 million small companies in the U.S. Of those businesses, 75% were operated by one person alone. However, the odds of success lasting longer than 5 years are limited. In 10 years only 1/3 of them remain in operation. Despite these statistics small to mid-size mature businesses flourish—like Apple and Hewlett Packard, were born in a garage. We all know how those companies turned out."

Before any business can be successful or become a legend, it must have a consistent profit or access to financing.

SBA states, "The average startup for most business in the U.S. is about 30,000." (Small Business

Administration, n.d.)You can use the cost calculator provided by Entrepreneur.com. This number may seem high, but there is a wide range of options when it comes to financing startups. Below is a list of ways for a new business to raise money:

- Self-Financing: Using personal funds to start a business.
    - a) Personal savings
    - b) Sell personal assets
    - c) Credit cards
    - d) Second mortgage or home equity loan
    - e) Bank loan
    - f) Cash retirement accounts
- Friends or Family
- Small Business Admin Loans (SBA)
    - a) Loan program
    - b) Microloans
- Venture Capital
- Angel Investors:
    - a) Go4Funding
    - b) MicroVentures
    - c) Tech Coast Angels
    - d) Investors' Circle
    - e) Golden Seeds LLC

f) Band of Angels
g) Hyde Park Angels
h) Alliance of Angels
i) Angel Capital Association

- Crowdfunding
    a) EquityNet
    b) SeedUps
    c) peerbackers
    d) RocketHub
    e) SeedInvest
- Peer to Peer Loans
    a) Incubators
    b) Idealab

In conclusion, preparing a start-up business requires an extensive amount of planning and effort. It is an option that must be weighed carefully, considering all the benefits and downsides of the funding options. Many small businesses are started using multiple sources of funding, which allows some flexibility. In the event of an unexpected financial expense, the funding will be there to solve the problem. Fortunately, the amount of new fund sources is growing constantly, making it an even better time to start your own business.

Outsourcing

One way to manage a lack of employees or a high workload is to outsource labor. This has been a common practice for many years, although with the invention of the Internet, outsourcing has taken on new levels of profitability. It has become a great alternative to many companies who need small important jobs done in a short period.

Outsourcing simply means the practice of obtaining goods or services from an alternative source, usually outside your home country. The costs will vary depending on the job. Companies outsource for several reasons, but two of the biggest motivations are lower costs and profitability. The strategy is very helpful to small business owners who have a limited budget and need to have quality work done for a lower price.

Leadership Team and Communication

"Few things help an individual more than to place responsibility on them and let them know you trust them" ***Booker T. Washington.***

One key role of any leader is the ability to use effective communication. The messages must come from respect and trust, and this is what separates a good leader from a poor leader. Interactions need to be frequent and constructive, which will encourage a healthy, productive workplace.

Positive communication is important in any area of life; between family members, spouses, co-workers, bosses, etc. Without conversation, productivity slows, and spats over expectations increase. Below are ways to create effective communication habits in the workplace:

1. Open meetings
2. Emails
3. One on one conversations
4. Amenable atmosphere
5. Communication training
6. Confidence in the staff
7. Simple clarifying expectations
8. Use visuals
9. Listen to feedback
10. Use positive body language
11. Eliminate unnecessary repetition
12. Maintain a positive tone

13. Use humor when appropriate
14. Be articulate
15. Give positive affirmations

The goal of any good leader should be to communicate in an effective manner that is respectful by constructively sharing your thoughts and feelings with the team or staff. The next step of good communication is the ability to listen to feedback from the team and staff. Then make the appropriate decision based on the proper information.

Chapter Nineteen:

Setting Up a Business

According to Small Business, "There are more than 28 million small businesses in the United States, making up a whopping 99.7 percent of all U.S. businesses, according to the Small Business Administration. When you consider some of the most popular reasons to start a business, including having a unique business idea, designing a career that has the flexibility to grow with you, working toward financial independence, and investing in yourself — it's no wonder that small businesses are everywhere." (Small Business, n.d.)

Below are four steps to start a business:

Step 1: Research

Whether you have already identified a business idea or not, take some time to research your options.

- Weight the odds

- Does the idea have the potential to succeed?
- Do you have the resources to start this endeavor?

You will need to run your business idea through a validation process before you go any further. The only way a small business will prosper is if it can solve a problem, fulfill a demand, or create something the market needs.

Luckily, several options are available to identify the answer, including focus groups and even trial and error. As you explore the market, some of the questions you should answer include:

- Is there a need for your anticipated products/services?
- Who needs it?
- Are there other companies offering similar products/services now?
- What is the competition like?
- How will your business fit into the market?

Step 2: Plan

A business plan is the blueprint of any business start-up. Once you have created this plan, the business can form its identity. The good news is that there are different types of business plans for different types of businesses.

If the plan is to seek financial support from an investor, a traditional plan must be in place. Business plans are generally thorough and have a common set of sections that investors and banks look for when they are validating your idea. Otherwise, a simple one-page business plan will be sufficient. In fact, using notepad in Microsoft can hold a plan that will be improved upon over time. Having any plan in writing is a great way to start.

Step 3: Plan Finances

Many people are afraid to start a business due to a lack of finances, but in this digital age, many options that did not exist before the Internet have opened.

Create a budget planner that includes all start-up costs such as licenses and permits, equipment, legal fees, insurance, branding, market research, inventory, trademarking, grand opening events, property leases, etc. Include expenses you anticipate over the next year, like rent, utilities, marketing and advertising, production, supplies, travel expenses, employee salaries, your salary, etc. It is important to be realistic about your profits, so plan for the yearly investment, but hope for the best.

Once the numbers are calculated, below are some ways to fund the small business:

- Financing
- Small business loans
- Small business grants
- Angel investors
- Crowdfunding

Bootstrapping is another way to fund the business. Start with a small amount and use it as necessary. However, you figure out the plan, so use the methods that best fit your needs.

Step 4: Create a Business Structure

Your small business can be a sole proprietorship, a partnership, a limited liability company (LLC), or a corporation. The business entity you choose will impact many factors, from your business name to your liability, to how you file your taxes. As the business grows the initial structure can be adjusted.

Depending on the complexity of your business, it may be worth investing in a consultation from an attorney or CPA to ensure you are making the right structure choice for your business.

Business Structure

There are 6 common business structures:

- Sole Proprietorship
- Partnership
- Corporation
- S Corporation
- Limited Liability (LLC)
- Limited Liability (LLP)

The tax implications vary greatly, so choose wisely. Be sure it matches your business needs.

Sole Proprietorship

A sole proprietor is someone who owns an unincorporated business by himself or herself. However, if you are the sole member of a domestic limited liability company (LLC), you are not a sole proprietor if you elect to treat the LLC as a corporation. If you intend to work alone, this structure may be the answer.

The tax aspects of a sole proprietorship are appealing because the expenses and your income from the business are included on your income tax return, Form 1040. Profits and losses are recorded on a form called Schedule C, which is filled with a 1040. The amount from Schedule C is then transferred to your tax return. However, the self-employment tax percentages are high, so prepare for the expense during tax season. It does offer business losses that may offset income earned from other sources.

The federal government permits you to pay estimated taxes in four equal amounts throughout the year on the 15th of April, June, September, and January. In a sole proprietorship, earnings are taxed only once, unlike other business structures. Also, you will have complete control over your business - you make all the decisions.

Raising money for a sole proprietorship can be difficult. Banks and other financing sources may be reluctant to make business loans to sole proprietorships. In most cases, you will have to depend on your financing sources, such as savings, home equity, or family loans.

Partnership

Business ventures operated by several individuals should consider a partnership. Partnerships come in two varieties: general partnerships and limited partnerships. In a general partnership, the partners manage the company and assume responsibility for the partnership's debts and other obligations. A limited partnership has both general and limited partners. The general partners own and operate the business and assume liability for the partnership, while the limited partners serve as investors only; they have no control over the company and are not subject to the same liabilities as the general partners.

If you don't expect to have many passive investors, a limited partnership is usually not the best choice for new business due to all the filings and administrative complexities. If you have two or more partners who want to be actively involved, a general partnership would be much easier to form.

One of the major advantages of a partnership is the tax treatment it enjoys. A partnership does not pay tax on its income but "passes through" any profits or losses to the individual partners. At tax time, the partnership must file a tax return (Form 1065) that reports its income and loss to the IRS. Besides, each partner reports his or her share of income and loss on Schedule K-1 of Form 1065.

The personal liability if you use a general partnership in the business requires each general partner to act on behalf of the partnership, take out loans and make decisions that will affect and be binding on all the partners (if the partnership agreement permits). Partnerships require legal accounting services and usually are more expensive to operate.

Corporation

In general, a corporation is formed under state law by the filing of articles of incorporation with the state. The state must generally date-stamp the articles before they are effective. You may wish to consult the law of the state in which the organization is incorporated. A corporation is an independent legal entity, separate from its owners, and as such it requires complying with more regulations and tax requirements.

One of the benefits of incorporation is liability protection. The business is its own identity; in other words, the business pays taxes and you are an employee. A corporation also can retain some of its profits without the owner paying tax on them.

Corporations can raise money, and sell the stock, either common or preferred, to raise funds. Corporations also continue indefinitely, even if one of the shareholders dies, sells the shares, or becomes disabled. The corporate structure, however, comes with several downsides. A major one is higher costs. Corporations are formed under the laws of each state with their own set of regulations. You will probably need the assistance of an attorney to guide you. In addition, because a corporation must follow more complex rules and regulations than a partnership or sole proprietorship, it requires more accounting and tax preparation services.

Corporations also pay double taxes on business earnings. They are subject to corporate tax with both state and federal, but the shareholders that are paid dividends are taxed on the individual tax rates.

A corporation is not required to pay tax on earnings paid as reasonable compensation, and it can deduct the payments as a business expense. However, the

IRS has limits on what it believes to be reasonable compensation.

S Corporation

S corporations are corporations that elect to pass corporate income, losses, deductions, and credits through to their shareholders for federal tax purposes. Shareholders of S corporations report the flow-through of income and losses on their tax returns and are assessed tax at their individual income tax rates. This allows S corporations to avoid double taxation on corporate income. S corporations are responsible for tax on certain built-in gains and passive income at the entity level.

If S corporations don't have inventory, they can use the cash method for accounting. The process is simplified. Income is taxable when received and expenses are deductible when paid.

S corporations can also have up to 100 shareholders. This option allows them to have more investors, and in essence gain more investors.

The downside is they are subject to many of the same rules as corporations, which means higher legal and tax services. They also must file articles of incorporation, hold directors and shareholders meetings, keep corporate minutes, and allow shareholders to vote on major corporate decisions.

The major difference between a regular corporation and an S corporation is that S corporations can only issue one class of stock. This can hamper a company's ability to raise any capital.

Limited Liability Company

S corporations are corporations that elect to pass corporate income, losses, deductions, and credits through to their shareholders for federal tax purposes. Shareholders of S corporations report the flow-through of income and losses on their tax returns and are assessed tax at their individual income tax rates. This allows S corporations to avoid double taxation on corporate income. S corporations are responsible for tax on certain built-in gains and passive income at the entity level.

Yes, they are similar however, an LLC offers owners more benefits than S corporations. The shareholder limit is 100, plus any member is allowed full partaking in business operations.

The set-up of an LLC requires filing articles of incorporation with the secretary of state but is generally much easier than a corporation. Some state statutes stipulate that the company must dissolve after 30 years. Technically, the company dissolves when a member dies, quits, or retires.

With a limited liability partnership, members are liable for their malpractice insurance. The legal form works well for those involved in professional practice, such as physicians.

Once settled on a business structure, the circumstances that make one type of business organization favorable are always subject to changes in the laws. It makes sense to reassess your form of business from time to time to make sure you are using the one that provides the most benefits.

Step 5: Pick and Register Business Name

A major factor in starting a business is choosing the right name. It plays a role in almost every area of business. Choose wisely!

After you have chosen a name, the next step is checking to see if it's trademarked or currently in use. The name must be registered, and a sole proprietor needs to register the name with the state or county clerk. Corporations, LLCs, or limited partnerships typically register their business name when the formation paperwork is filed.

Once the name is registered, search for the domain name. It may be best to check on available domain names ahead of time. It is recommended to have three different options in case the first choice is not available. Online presence in this digital age is imperative.

Step 6: Get Licenses and Permits

Any business start-up requires paperwork. Depending on the choice of business the licensing or permits will vary. The location will also determine the type of paperwork. Always research what is needed ahead of time to help eliminate any surprises.

Step 7: Choose an Accounting System

Any business must have an accounting system in place beforehand. However, for small businesses, this is extremely important. The system will manage a budget, set rates and pricing, conduct business, and file taxes. If you are unsure of the mechanics, the option to hire an accountant is always a good alternative.

Step 8: Set Up Business Location

All businesses need a dedicated location of operation. Not only for tax purposes but to maintain a professional atmosphere. Once the location is decided, then it's time to get all the equipment involved in running the business. Equipment can be purchased or leased.

Step 9: Initiate a Team

Once all the particulars are completed, it's time to either hire full-time employees or part-time staff members. The Small Business Administration has an excellent guide to hiring your first employee that is useful for new small business owners.

If you are not hiring employees but instead are outsourcing work to independent contractors, now is the time to work with an attorney to get your independent contractor agreement in place and start your search.

In conclusion, if you are a true solopreneur, you may not need employees or contractors. Although, having a support team is important. The staff can be mentors, friends, or small business coaches, whoever services the purpose of your business needs.

Step 10: Business Promotion

Now that the hard initial work is done, it is time to start attracting clients or customers. The process begins with writing a unique selling proposition. Create a marketing plan! Without income, the business won't survive. Then, explore as many small business marketing ideas as possible to promote the business most effectively.

What is Copyrighting?

A copyright is the protection of an original work of authorship, both published and unpublished. It is used by writers, musicians, artists, and others to protect their work from unauthorized commercial use.

Understanding Copyright Protection

Automatically acquire the copyright of your work the moment you create it.

Your work is automatically protected by copyright when it is "fixed in a tangible form" like a piece of writing or drawing on a piece of paper. This means the U.S. copyright laws apply to your work as soon as you produce it, write it, record it, or draw it. An idea or invention can only be protected when it is in tangible form. Write the idea out in detail.

In situations where you authorized a person to record your words, you hold the 'first of record,' as you remain the author. But it would be advisable to have them sign a non-disclosure agreement.

U.S. law prohibits copyrighting a recording of a live public performance unless you obtain permission from the performers. You could be sued for infringement for making it or sharing it online or anywhere else.

Understand the difference between a copyright, a patent, and a trademark. Copyright protects original works of authorship created by you. However, a patent protects inventions and useful discoveries. A trademark protects distinctive words, phrases, symbols, sounds, and designs. Trademarks identify and distinguish the source of the goods (and services) of one party from those of another party.

It is important to know what types of work are protected by copyrights. Copyright protects original, tangible work you have created including things like writings, drawings, photographs, books, and poems.

It also protects:

- Movies and soundtracks
- Choreography and dramatic works
- Songs and sound recordings
- Artistic works like paintings and sculptures and computer software programs
- Architecture plans and drawings

Copyrights do not protect an idea or something expressed verbally. Copyright also does not protect:

- Facts or concepts
- Domain names
- Slogans
- Systems or methods of operation
- Names (including band names) or titles
- Works created by the US government
- Works in the "public domain", i.e., having an expired or void US copyright.

The ownership of copyright affords an exclusive right to make copies of protected work. An owner can sell, print, or distribute the work legally. Copyright also allows you to create adaptations, translations, or derivative pieces from your work, and to perform your work.

However, the exclusive rights come with limitations, such as fair use, first sale, or certain educational and non-profit uses.

Anyone can choose to authorize others, via license, to exercise some or all your exclusive rights either for compensation or as a courtesy. The prevention of others from making personal copies is not prohibited. Only the use of commercial use can be regulated.

Work for hire can be made for an employer or a client under an independent contract. The law determines who the original owner of the copyright is, which also determines the copyright duration. If a work is created by an employee as part of their work, then the employer is considered "the author" and owns the copyright.

If an independent contractor is hired, make sure the copyright agreement is determined before the start of the project. Complex issues arise when collaborating with others in a jointly authored work. Research when copyright protection ends.

You must know when copyright protection ends. For works created in 1978 or later, copyright generally lasts for the duration of the last living author's life, plus an additional 70 years. If the work was made for hire, anonymous, or created under a pseudonym, the copyright lasts for 95 years from the first publication or 120 years from the creation.

Copyright will last beyond the normal lifespan of a person, so the necessary paperwork should be initiated while the person is alive. The material should be kept with a will or estate plan. Ownership can also be transferred by contacting the US copyright office.

Until 1972, sound recordings were not protected by copyrights, but may be protected under various state laws until 2067. Foreign copyright laws vary.

Registering a Copyright

1) Copyrights are a consideration for anyone, but not necessary. They can be registered through the U.S. Copyright office. Several reasons apply for copyright registration:
    - A registered copyright is a matter of public record.
    - Registered copyright holders receive a certificate of registration from the U.S. Copyright Office.
    - Registration must be done to bring a lawsuit on a related infringement.

- Any works registered may be eligible for statutory damages and attorney's fees.

The process must be completed within the first 5 years of publication. Otherwise, the burden falls on the author to prove ownership.

2) Copyrights can be registered online very easily. Visit the U.S. Copyright Office's online registration site. You will need to register an account with the office to start your application. A digital version of the work must be provided, or you can request a shipping label.

   Then, pay the filing fees and submit all works. You can also pay the filing fee online and submit your application.

3) Register your copyright by mail. If you chose to register by mail, the U.S. Copyright Office website can provide the proper paperwork. If you are registering a novel, select the Literary Form (Form TX), a music or voice recording, select the Sound Recording Form (Form SR).

   Print the form and refer to the guide as to the number of copies that are required. Make a copy or copies of your copyrighted work.

Once the application is received, you will get a certificate in the mail, or online if that route is chosen. If for any reason the application is rejected, a notification of the issue will be mailed. You will have a chance to appeal.

Part Three: Protecting a Copyright

1) Place notices on all copyrighted work. A notice is helpful in case of infringement. A copyright notice may also make it easier to collect damages in any potential infringement lawsuit.

   A copyright notice should contain the word "copyright" or a "c" in a circle (©), along with the date of first publication and the name of the owner of the copyright

   If someone copies a copyrighted work, send a cease-and-desist letter before taking any legal action. The letter must include details of the issue, and ask the party to stop their illegal actions. From there if the issue persists, consult an attorney for further options.

Chapter Twenty:

Using Rumble

If you're tired of censorship, cancel culture, and the erosion of civil liberties, Rumble is a great option.

The online video management company was founded in 2013 and has enjoyed growing success with millions of users migrating in response to YouTube's increased censorship of its users.

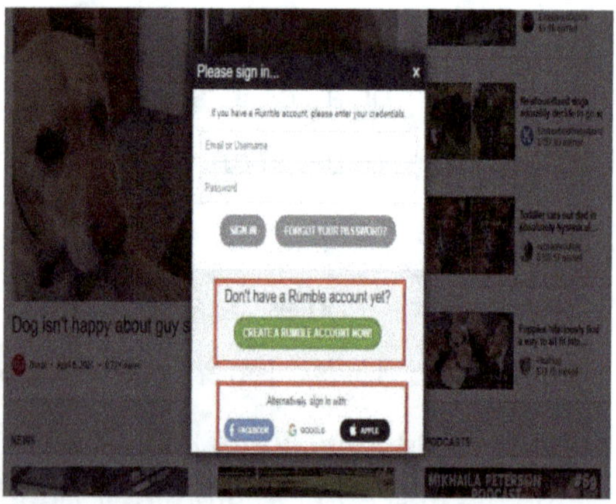

Its CEO, Chris Pavlovski, has vowed to never censor political discussions on the platform or adopt policies that dictate editorial policy.

He has also written that Rumble wants to "provide an open platform where everyone can participate and create videos without subjective restrictions."

Rumble has partnered with Truthsocial.com coming in the first quarter of 2022.

Political content is popular on the platform, with conservative influencers and commentators such as Dan Bongino (who is also an investor), Dinesh D'Souza, HodgeTwins, and Bannon's War Room (Steve Bannon) among the most viewed creators on the platform.

Approach to content moderation and community Pavlovski has stated that "Rumble is not here to be an arbiter of truth and has been highly critical of YouTube's increased censorship."

He directly criticized YouTube's growing censorship of scientific discussions and debates; its frequent policy changes that restrict what users are allowed to post. Its December 2020 ban on videos alleging "widespread fraud or errors" changed the 2020 US presidential election outcome.

Pavlovski responded to this YouTube ban on videos alleging widespread fraud or errors, which changed the election outcome by vowing that "Rumble will not adopt a policy like this."

The Rumble CEO has also publicly committed to respecting the rights of the Rumble community and welcomes debate among users. "We are not a publisher, and we respect the rights of our community to engage in debate, discussion, challenge opinion, and dialogue, even if one party feels that's wrong or incorrect," Pavlovski wrote in a statement to the Rumble community.

Video Discovery and Distribution Features

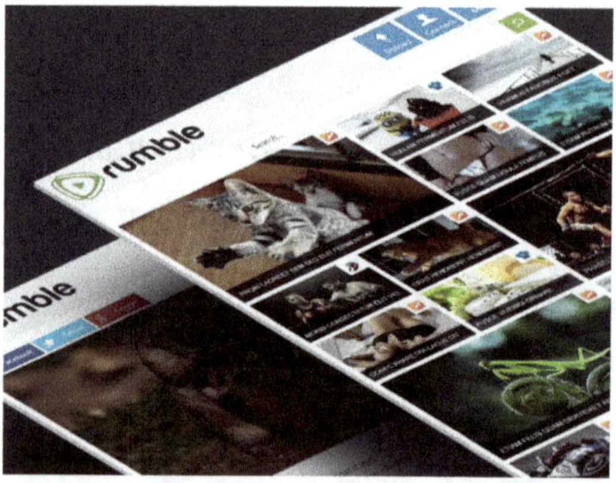

One of Rumble's most unique video discovery and distribution features is the Rumble feed, which is available in Rumble's mobile app. The feed presents a series of auto-play videos that you can "Rumble" (a positive vote similar to a "Like" or an upvote) or skip by swiping left or right.

Videos with the most Rumbles are placed on a "Battle Leaderboard", which is refreshed daily and can be viewed on both desktop and mobile. The Battle Leaderboard is a great video discovery and distribution feature but allows viewers to collect tickets that can be used to win a daily cash draw.

Subscriptions are another feature similar to subscriptions and follow on other social media apps. You can subscribe to channels or categories, and the latest videos from your subscriptions appear on the "My Feed" page.

Rumble also promotes videos via its "Editor Picks" page (which displays curated videos), "Trending" page (which highlights some of the most popular videos on Rumble), and its homepage categories (which showcase videos from several of Rumble's topic-based categories).

The videos on channel pages, the Editors Picks page, and the Trending page can also be sorted in various ways, including by most recent, most shared, most viewed, vitality, and date.

Native Monetization Options

Creators can monetize Rumble videos through three licensing options:

Rumble Video Player license: The video is monetized on Rumble.com. It is a non-exclusive license, which means you can still share the video on other platforms.

Exclusive Video Management license: Rumble takes care of the full distribution of the video across its networks, including Rumble.com, YouTube, and other third-party partners such as AOL, MSN, and Yahoo. This license has the potential to bring in the most revenue.

Video Management (excluding YouTube) license: This license is the same as the Exclusive Video Management license, except the videos, don't get distributed on YouTube.

If you don't want to monetize your videos, a Personal Use license is available. This license allows you to retain full control and all rights, with Rumble only retaining the license to show the video on Rumble.com. Videos with this license receive no promotion and are only available via a direct link.

Video Engagement and Sharing Features

Rumble has plenty of engagement and sharing features to stay up to date with videos and creators.

Videos on Rumble can be (liked/upvoted) or downvote videos and comments, share videos, embed videos, and comment on videos. You can also subscribe to channels and categories to stay up to date with videos from your favorite creators and on your favorite topics.

Each video page has a share button (which allows users to quickly share the video via several mediums) and an embed button (which gives you instant access to embed code and direct links for hosting or linking to the video off-site).

4K Video Support

Rumble supports HD video playback in up to 4K (2160p). You can also choose your preferred video quality with 360p, 480p, 720p, and 1080p playback available.

Customizable Notifications

Rumble offers a range of customizable email and in-app notifications for creators and viewers.

If using the mobile app, you can choose to be notified when a video is placed on the front page, or receive comments on videos, when your video is trending, and when other users comment on your comments, and more.

Notifications can be set up for daily, weekly, or monthly email notifications. These notifications are fully customizable and allow you to set up instant notifications for favorite categories and creators.

Additional Features

Rumble also has live streaming, playlists, and improved monetization.

Playlists are currently available when the Rumble Player is embedded on other sites.

Rumble plans to improve its monetization by building an internal ad platform similar to Facebook and Snapchat's ad system. This system should give Rumble more control over ads and improve user privacy.

Chapter Twenty-One:

Using BitChute

The video-sharing platform BitChute is a sharing social media site that uses peer-to-peer technology. As the users

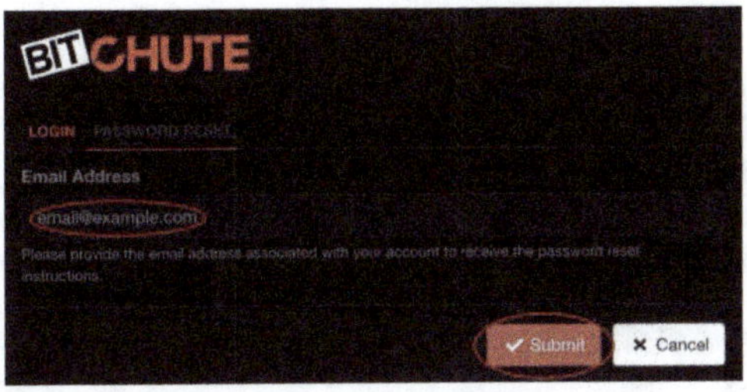

following increases, the base grows. BitChute offers many videos for users to watch, but the videos cannot be downloaded.

BitChute was launched on January 3, 2017, to host user-created videos. The platform runs on BitTorrent. A technology to share videos from one user to others.

The website is a YouTube alternative that allows free speech, void of censorship. Anyone can upload and start a BitChute account.

What Do BitTorrent and Peer-To-Peer Mean?

BitChute Founder Quoted, “The idea comes from seeing the increased levels of censorship by the large social media platforms in the last couple of years. Banning’s, demonetization, and tweaking algorithms to send certain content into obscurity and, wanting to do something about it.”

Peer-To-Peer is a Network of Users

In peer-to-peer file sharing, everybody who shares and downloads files acts as a node.

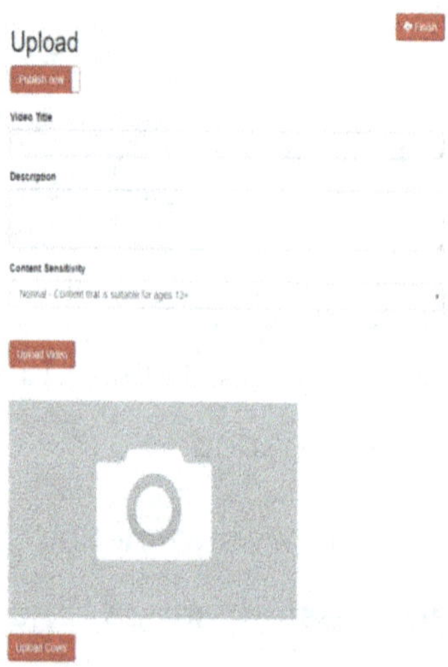

As people download the file from the first person, they share the file with other people and create a network with sharers and downloaders.

Files Spread Fast with Peer-To-Peer

Once enough people become nodes, there is pretty much no way to stop the file from being shared, unless you could somehow turn off everybody at once.

No central server or service is needed to keep things going, as only one person needs to start the sharing.

What Is BitTorrent?

The BitTorrent file-sharing protocol is one of the most popular ways to share files online using peer-to-peer. People use a BitTorrent client like QBittorrent or Transmission to share and download files.

How BitTorrent Works

Peers download files, and people seeders upload files back to the network. It is a good practice to seed after you finish downloading something.

What Are Lechers in BitTorrent?

People who download files and then immediately stop peer-to-peer sharing are called leechers, or referred to as a hit-and-run.

- Leecher can also refer to people who are still downloading a file and not uploading it yet.
- BitTorrent is Open-Source Software, such as GIMP, LibreOffice.

BitChute uses WebTorrent

BitChute uses a web-based BitTorrent client. WebTorrent is a BitTorrent client that runs in web browsers.

BitChute Shares Video Files

Using WebTorrent creates a file-sharing effect. There are no central servers, and the files come from other users.

Overview of How BitChute Works

BitChute users create channels and upload videos to the website. These users become peers for people to download, thereafter the videos are downloaded to watch. Those people become peers for other people.

Why BitChute?

Big Tech has been censoring users for years. People are looking for better alternatives. As an open platform, BitChute can offer another channel.

The BitChute team does not censor, it will be up to the users to filter out what they do not want to see. The policy gives people a safe place to make and post content. Therefore, people will not have to worry about their videos being silenced or moderated.

Can You Make Money with BitChute?

BitChute does not currently have a way to earn money from uploading videos, but the developer team promises this feature is coming.

Options to Make Money

- Receive cryptocurrency donations.
- Receive tips from viewers.

Chapter Twenty-Two:

Using FrankSpeech.com

"Free speech is one of the hallmarks of our Constitutional Republic, as enshrined in the Bill of Rights. It is no coincidence that nations with free speech also have a free enterprise system and freedom of religion. Inversely, nations that deny free speech tread upon the free enterprise system and freedom of religion. Americans want to remain free. Americans crave news and information that is not filtered through the radical worldview of today's liberal media intelligentsia, or deep state actors.

Frank, the voice of free speech, will be the platform for Americans who want to defend life, liberty, and all the freedoms that have marked America as the longest-running Constitutional Republic in the world. On this platform, you will find a home where you can post videos, Livestream television, distribute news and information, and find community and fellowship with like-minded Americans. Frank will be a home for major influencers, micro-influencers, to average Americans wanting to share the constitutional right of freedom of speech and freedom of expression. We hope you will join our community and let freedom ring." Mike Lindell

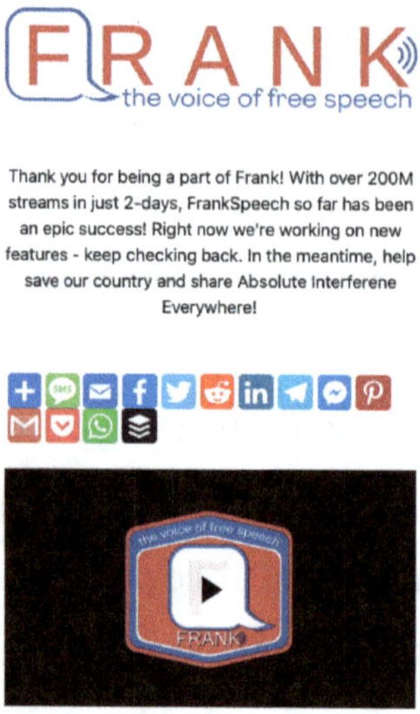

FrankSpeech.com 'The Voice of Free Speech' launched on April 19th, 2021. The platform had been in development for over four years, emerging after big tech began censoring many conservative individuals and businesses. Frankspeech.com is a static site that showcases the voices of everyday people. The site offers free speech to express users' views on different topics.

The website frankspeech.com offers Americans the opportunity to voice their opinions. Users can share videos, post information, news, live stream TV, and much more. Any user searching for a platform free from offensive posts or language, FrankSpeech has promised to maintain a Christian-based news source.

Sign up for FrankSpeech.com

1. Submit your mobile phone number to receive a text code confirming US citizenship. The page will

reload, and your data is now successfully submitted to FrankSpeech aka Frank.

How to use FrankSpeech.com

1. You can add FrankSpeech to your phone's home screen by following the below steps. The steps are for both IOS (iPad or iPhone) and Android users. You can add the app to chrome and safari.

Chapter Twenty-Three:

Using Brighteon

Brighteon was founded in 2018, to bring forth a free speech uncensored platform. The founder is Mike Adams, who owns several websites, such as Natural News and News Target. Although Brighteon is part of the Natural News Network.

The website generates revenue through online advertising, donations, and an online store that sells supplements and preparedness supplies.

In 2019 Brighteon.com emerged as an alternative outlet to YouTube. The platform provides all the necessary hosting for any video news outlet.

- Video uploading and transcoding into multiple bitrate renditions
- Affordable video storage (our new solution saves us 90% compared to our previous costs)
- Video playback across multiple devices and browsers

Sign up

1. Add email/username
2. Free to join
3. Upload videos

There are a few commonsense exceptions to the free speech nature of the platform, such as Brighteon is not appropriate for pornographic material, illegal material, snuff videos, etc. Brighteon complies with U.S. law, which means videos calling for violence against individuals, or that promote stalking behavior against individuals, etc.

Brighteon follows the same pattern as GAB, leading the way to free speech platforms. The goal is to provide a platform for all speech protected by the First Amendment, including speech that some people decide to categorize as "offensive."

Brighteon.com already hosts over 100,000 videos uploaded by thousands of users. Any platform that promotes free speech, Brighteon supports. In fact, moving forward, they are working with Gab on social media integration measures that are technically feasible.

How to Make Money on Social Media

Since the invention of the Internet, the ways people can make money have become limitless. One fantastic way to increase any income is social media. In fact, it can be very lucrative. Below are some outlets for making money through social media:

1. Endorse affiliate products
2. Create and promote information products
3. Sell products and services
4. Use visual media to promote your crafts
5. Offer coaching or consulting services
6. Join partner program

We have only listed a few ways to generate extra income using social media, and there are many more options. The important thing to remember is the process may not be easy to get started and it will take time to become financially beneficial, but don't give up and be persistent.

Public Relations

The public relations business has gotten a bad rap over the years because most people do not understand what it means or what the job entails. Public relations promote a client's product or services in a manner free of charge to unpaid audiences. The idea is to generate a public understanding of the business's skills and industry in which they work. Below are 5 things every public relations person should know:

1. Public relations are like storytelling
   a) Write and distribute press releases
   b) Write speeches
   c) Write pitches (less formal than press releases) about a firm and send them directly to journalists
   d) Create and execute special events designed for public outreach and media relations
   e) Conduct market research on the firm or the firm's messaging
   f) Expand business contacts via personal networking or attendance and sponsoring at events

   g) Write and blog for the web (internal or external sites)
   h) Create public relations crisis management strategies
   i) Design social media promotions and responses to negative opinions online
2. Public relations is different than advertising
3. Understand the nature of the news
   a) Create the story
   b) Follow a story
4. Social media cannot replace traditional media
5. It is possible to measure public relations

Media is Your Friend

Media is an essential part of marketing any business. If people do not know you exist, how can they become clients?

Below are 28 ways to help get media attention for your business:

1. Learn what media outlets are covering
2. Use email over the phone
3. Engage the right people

4. Schedule regular postings, stories, and engagement
5. Become the expert
6. Always be reachable
7. Create a resource center for your business
8. Tweet with followers
9. Take advantage of freebies
10. Plan special events in your local area and invite the media
11. Engage on social media platforms
12. Offer to review products that pertain to your business
13. Write a complete press release
14. Be a resource for clients or followers
15. Avoid buzzwords and tech jargon
16. Use bullet points and pitches
17. Don't overhype
18. Do something unique
19. Create research
20. Give shout outs
21. Invite the media to your special events
22. Start with blogs of media outlets
23. Create your media shortlist

24. Attend community events where the press may be present
25. Watch publications with smaller and more targeted readerships
26. Hold a fundraising drive
27. Carefully choose your backdrop
28. Learn from your experience

Social Media Marketing Tools

- **MavSocial** is a scheduling tool for social media (my personal favorite)
- **Sensible** is a scheduling tool for social media
- **Buffer** is a scheduling tool for social media.
- **Buzzsumo** is a research tool that tells you how your content is doing and who's spreading the word.
- **Missinglettr** helps you automate the process of creating social content by scraping your blog post content and creating a year's worth of social content for you. It makes nine individual posts dripped out to your social channels over a year.
- **MeetEdgar** is your handy automated content manager.
- **Hootsuite** handles multiple social media accounts, bringing them under one login into a single dashboard.
- **Mention** is an extremely comprehensive social listening tool.

- **Sumo** has a whole suite of useful traffic and social media tools that can help improve your marketing strategy.
- **IFTTT** means if this, then that. This tool lets you set up rules that make running your social media marketing empire much easier.
- **Zapier** is another tool that encourages automation and does share some similarities with IFTTT.
- **Bitly** is a link shortener, taking lengthy URLs and shrinking them into much smaller ones.
- **Sprout Social** provides engagement, publishing, analytics, and team collaboration tools.
- **Design Wizard** is another tool that's good for making visual content, with a reasonably simple and intuitive interface.
- **Socialbakers** enables brands to work smart on social media through artificial intelligence (AI) to understand audience behavior.
- **Post Planner** makes it easy for you to find and share content consistently to get predictable, considerable, and remarkable results on social media.

- **Sprinklr** is a four-in-one social media marketing platform that can help you with social engagement, social advocacy, customer care, and social advertising.
- **SocialFlow** allows you to schedule your posts when your target audience is active and engage in real-time.
- **Brand24** gives you insights on what people are saying online about your brand. This tool helps you track your competitors, too.
- **Tracx** is the only social listening tool that provides an all-in-one solution that captures the full conversation.
- **ShortStack** has positioned itself as the most powerful marketing platform for contests and giveaways.
- **Canva** makes it easy to create gorgeous infographics, cover images, and thumbnails for your social media accounts.

Social Media Directory

A.

Abandonment rate: The percentage of social customer service issues that customers abandon before they are resolved.

Algorithm: A rules-based procedure for making calculations or solving problems—they're everywhere in computer science! In social media, constantly shifting algorithms control which contents its users see (and don't see), as well as what topics and hashtags are trending.

Analytics: Data, and the patterns found in that data, are often used to make marketing or advertising decisions. A website or application gathers data for its analytics using a cookie or other tracking tag that monitors users' behavior. The tag activates when users begin their visits and then stores data about what pages they visited, what actions they completed, and how they interacted with different elements such as clicking on buttons or performing a search.

Authenticity: The practice of using a tone and voice online that expresses who you are. For brands, being open and authentic on social media means a great deal to those who want to engage with you. Conveying your brand's values through your content and replies, and interacting with followers in a way that's relatable and human, all contribute to your sense of authenticity.

B.

Bio: The small portion of any digital profile that tells new or prospective followers who you are. All social platforms offer space to write a bio. It's the first thing users see when they discover your profile, and a good one can greatly improve how often you show up in keyword searches.

Bitly: Bitly is a free URL shortening service that provides statistics for the links users share online. Bitly is often used to condense long URLs to make them easier to share on social networks such as Twitter.

Block: A Twitter feature that allows you to prevent another user from:

- Following you
- Sliding into your DMs
- Adding you to their lists
- Tagging you in photos

Blocking a troublesome or harassing user allows you some peace—if they mention you, those tweets won't appear in your notifications, and the user receives a message letting them know they've been blocked.

BoardReader: BoardReader is a free search engine that allows users to search for keywords only in posts and titles of online forums, a popular form of social networking.

Bookmarking: Bookmarking online follows the same idea of placing a bookmark in a physical publication - you're simply marking something you found important, enjoyed, or want to continue reading later. The only difference online is that it's happening through websites using one of the various bookmarking services available, such as Pocket, or right within your browser.

Brand advocate: A customer who loves your organization so much that they become an extension of your marketing team. They evangelize your products or services without being asked and can become even more valuable if you connect with them directly to engage and empower them.

Brandjacking: The hijacking of a person or organization's name or likeness to promote an agenda or damage the target's reputation. Brandjackers don't hack their targets' social accounts; instead, they assume a target's online identity with fake accounts, promoted hashtags, and satirical marketing campaigns.

C.

Chatbot: A type of bot that lives in messaging apps (such as Facebook Messenger) and uses artificial intelligence to perform tasks via simulated conversation. A chatbot can be used for customer service, data collection, and more. Facebook is one of the leaders in chatbot integration.

Click-through rate (CTR): A common metric for reporting on the number of people who viewed a piece of content then took an action, such as clicking on an ad or link. CTR is most commonly used for pay-per-click advertising and other performance-driven channels. The general philosophy is that the higher your CTR, the more effective your marketing is.

Community management: The practice of developing relationships around a common interest, done by monitoring and engaging with those who engage with the common interest. The goal is to nurture relationships so that the community acts as advocates on behalf of the common interest.

Competitor sentiment: The practice of monitoring how users feel about other organizations in your space through social media monitoring. Whether positive or negative, this intel can provide important context that helps you to make strategic business decisions to stay ahead of the competition.

Connections: The LinkedIn equivalent of a GAB 'friend' is a 'connection.' Because LinkedIn is a social networking site, the people you are connecting with are not necessarily people you are friends with, but rather professional contacts that you've met, heard speak, done business with, or know through another connection. Connections are categorized by 1st degree, 2nd degree, and 3rd degree.

Content curation: The process of scouring the Internet for the best, most relevant content for an audience and then presenting it to them in a meaningful way. Unlike content marketing, content curation doesn't involve creating new content. Instead, it's about creating value for your audience by saving them time and effort. There's no shortage of content out there, but not all of it is worth reading. Organizing relevant content into pinboards, newsletters, or weekly roundups can help you build an audience and demonstrate your subject matter expertise.

Content management system (CMS): An online application that allows you to draft, edit, share, schedule, and index your content. Popular web content management systems have polished interfaces that allow you to publish content without knowing code. Hootsuite is a CMS.

Content marketing: The practice of attracting and retaining customers through the creation and distribution of valuable content, such as videos, white papers, guides, and infographics. Marketers hope to earn customer loyalty and influence decisions by publishing useful, entertaining, or educational content.

Conversion: A positive action taken on a website. The action demonstrates that the visitor is "raising their hand" and becoming a lead or customer. Sales are just one type of conversion; other examples include webinar registrations, newsletter signups, and gated-content downloads. Once a conversion takes place—usually involving the capture of a name and email address—a lead can be nurtured into a customer. In social marketing, conversion tracking is crucial to properly attribute revenue to social media efforts.

Cost per click (CPC): The terms pay-per-click (PPC) and cost-per-click (CPC) are sometimes used interchangeably, sometimes as distinct terms. When used as distinct terms, **PPC** indicates *payment* based on click-throughs, while **CPC** indicates *measurement* of cost on a per-click basis for contracts not based on click-throughs.

Creative Commons: Creative Commons is a nonprofit corporation dedicated to making it easier for people to share and build upon the work of others, consistent with the rules of copyright. It provides free licenses and other legal tools to mark creative work with the freedom the creator wants it to carry, so others can share, remix, use commercially, or any combination thereof.

Crowdsourcing: Leveraging your online community to assist in services, content, and ideas. Business applications for crowdsourcing include getting your audience to help translate your product or asking industry experts to contribute tips and tracks for an upcoming blog post.

D.

Dashboard: In a social relationship platform, a single screen where marketers can view their feeds, see and interact with ongoing conversations, monitor social trends, access analytics, and more.

Delicious: Delicious is a free online bookmarking service that lets users save website addresses publicly and privately online so they can be accessed from any device connected to the internet and shared with friends.

Digg: Digg is a social news website that allows members to submit and vote for articles. Articles with the most votes appear on the homepage of the site and subsequently are seen by the largest portion of the site's membership, as well as other visitors.

Direct message: A private Twitter or Instagram message. Direct messages can be sent only to Twitter and Instagram users who are already following you—and you can receive direct messages only from users you follow unless you have opted in to receiving direct messages from anyone in your user settings.

Disappearing content: Content that vanishes after a set amount of time (such as Snapchat, Facebook Stories, and Instagram Stories).

Display ad: Typically, small visual advertisements that are shown on websites. Common formats include images, Flash, video, and audio. They can also be text-based (for example, Google AdWords lets you build text-based display ads). In general, display ads are used for large audience-based media buys or retargeting.

E.

Embedded media: Digital media that is displayed outside of its native setting, such as within another piece of content (e.g., a GIF embedded into a Facebook comment, or a YouTube video shared in a Tweet).

Endorsement: An endorsement on LinkedIn refers to an instance in which another LinkedIn user recognizes you for one of the skills you have listed on your profile.

Engagement: Talking to, messaging, or otherwise interacting with other people on social networks. Engagement broadly encompasses many types of actions, from commenting on Instagram posts to producing a Facebook Live show with an open Q&A. Engagement is central to any social media strategy.

Engagement rate: The percentage of users who saw your social media post and took some kind of action (clicked the link, replied, shared, retweeted, etc.). The engagement rate is a valuable metric to gauge the success of your social media messaging. Twitter Analytics provides in-depth engagement rate data for every Tweet you send.

Eventbrite: Eventbrite is a provider of online event management and ticketing services. Eventbrite is free if your event is free. If you sell tickets to your event, Eventbrite collects a fee per ticket.

F.

Favorite: An indication that someone likes your Tweet, given by clicking the heart icon.

Feed: The social media data format that provides users with a steady stream of updates and information.

Filter: A photographic effect that can be applied to images before publishing them, from simple black-and-white or sepia to those ubiquitous flower crowns and puppy ears. Available on Instagram, Snapchat, Facebook Messenger, and many other apps with camera integrations, the popularity of filters has resulted in the hashtag #nofilter, a proud declaration that your latest photo is unedited.

First response time: The time it takes a company to give its first response to a customer's comment or inquiry on social media. This can be a key performance indicator for social customer service because even if the issue is not resolved immediately, a quick first response can demonstrate that a company is listening and willing to help.

Follow Friday (#ff) - Follow Friday is a trend via the hashtag #ff every Friday on Twitter. Users select other usernames and tweet them with #ff in their post, meaning they recommend following those Twitter users. There is debate about whether this trend is past its prime.

Follower: A Twitter user who has subscribed to your Twitter feed to see your tweets in their feed.

Followers-to-following ratio: The ratio of your social media followers to those you are following. In an ideal world, you have more followers than users you are following.

Friendship page: A page that tells the story of a relationship between two people connected on Facebook. Facebook Friendship pages display a variety of content, including photos that both people are tagged in together, public messages that they have exchanged, and their mutual friends and interests.

G.

Geotagging: Adding a specific location to a photo, video, or social media message. The ubiquity of GPS-enabled smartphones has made geotagging a core aspect of social media.

Geotargeting: A feature on many social media platforms that allows users to share their content with geographically defined audiences. Instead of sending a generic message for the whole world to see, you can refine the messaging and language of your content to better connect with people in specific cities, countries, and regions. You can also filter your audience by language.

GIF: Pronounced "gif," with a hard G, no matter what the actual creator of the GIF says. An acronym for Graphics Interchange Format, which refers to a file format that supports both static and animated images. GIFs rose to popularity as a way to react on social media without words.

H.

Hashtag: A word or phrase preceded by the "#" sign. Hashtags are a simple way to mark the topic (or topics) of social media messages and make them discoverable to people with shared interests. On most social networks, clicking a hashtag will reveal recently published messages with that hashtag. Hashtags first emerged on Twitter as a user-created phenomenon and is now used on almost every other social media platform.

Header image: A header image refers to the large photo displayed at the top of your profile on GETTR. The header image is also commonly referred to as the banner image on LinkedIn or the cover image on GAB.

Home: Often, the first page you see when you sign into your social media account. It contains a constantly updating timeline or feed of the user activity and news stories in your network.

I.

Impressions: An impression refers to a way in which marketers and advertisers keep track of every time an ad is "fetched" and counted.

Inbound marketing: A data-backed approach to attracting customers to web properties with relevant and helpful content. This content is discovered through channels like search engines and social media.

Influencer: A social media user with a significant audience who can drive awareness about a trend, topic, company, or product. From a marketer's perspective, the ideal influencer is also a passionate brand advocate. Successful influencer strategies usually involve the coordination of an organization's marketing, customer service, and public relations teams.

Influencer marketing: A strategy where a business collaborates with an influential person on social media to promote a product, service, or campaign. Think of it as micro-celebrity endorsements, designed for the digital age.

Instagram: A free online photo-sharing app that allows for the addition of several filters, editing, and sharing options.

Instant messaging (IM): A form of real-time, direct text-based communication between two or more people. More advanced instant messaging software clients also allow enhanced modes of communication, such as live voice or video calling.

K.

Key performance indicator (KPI): A metric that defines whether a marketing campaign or other initiative has succeeded or failed. KPIs for a social media marketing campaign might include brand mentions, replies, and retweets, or click-throughs to your website from individual posts.

L.

Like: Popularized digitally by Facebook—though derived from the dictionary definition—an understood expression of support for content. Along with shares, comments, and favorites, likes can be tracked as proof of engagement.

LinkedIn endorsement: A connection's recognition of another person's skill, such as content marketing, web programming, or cake baking. Endorsements, a form of social proof, boost your credibility through third-party confirmation that you have the skills you say you have. Users can endorse the skills of only their first-degree LinkedIn connections.

LinkedIn Publishing: LinkedIn's publishing platform functions as a place where members can publish long-form posts that relate to their professional interests and expertise. While this capability used to be limited to LinkedIn influencers only, the platform was opened to everyone in 2014.

LinkedIn SlideShare: An online social network for sharing presentations and documents. Users can favorite and embed presentations as well as share them on other social networks such as LinkedIn, Twitter, and Facebook.

LinkedIn recommendation: A written compliment from a connection that you can display on your LinkedIn profile to impress hiring managers, potential clients, and the 428 conference attendees you carpet-bombed with your business card. There's no limit to how many recommendations you can give or request, but remember that the most authentic recommendations come from people that you've worked with. If you receive a lackluster recommendation that you would rather not display, you can easily hide it from your profile. You can also edit, remove, or hide recommendations of your own LinkedIn connections at any time.

Live streaming: The act of delivering content over the Internet in real-time.

M.

Marketing automation: A combination of tactics and technology platforms that enable the automatic delivery of personalized content to prospects and customers through a variety of online channels. The idea behind marketing automation is giving website visitors and leads the information they need when they need it—and doing so at scale, which is where the automation comes in.

Marketing automation isn't about blindly scheduling content. Ideally, marketers will segment and score their marketing contacts, then nurture those potential customers with carefully tailored and timed messaging to move them toward an eventual purchase.

Solid social media marketing can attract new inbound leads, providing fuel for the marketing automation engine. Marketers can also make that engine more efficient by using social media data to learn more about their leads over time.

Mention: The act of tagging another user's handle or account name in a social media message. Mentions typically trigger a notification for that user and are a key part of what makes social media "social." A properly formatted mention also allows your audience to click through to the bio or profile of the user in question.

Microblogging: Publishing smaller, more frequent quantities of content to platforms such as Minds or MeWe.

Multichannel attribution: An analytics tactic aimed at better understanding how customers discover, evaluate, and purchase your products or services.

When people buy products, they rarely complete a purchase in one step. For example, they might hear about a brand in a tweet, later see a banner ad for the product, then perform a Google search, and then, many days later, finally visit the website to purchase.

Multichannel attribution attempts to give relative value to each of these channels, treating each channel as a contributor to a customer's eventual purchase. The goal: to better understand the process by which your customers develop a holistic understanding of how each marketing channel.

N.

News feed: A news feed is a feed full of news. On MeWe, the News Feed is the homepage of users' accounts where they can see all the latest updates from their friends. The news on most social media platforms is called the timeline.

Notification: A message or update sharing new social media activity. For example, if somebody likes one of your Instagram photos you can receive a notification on your phone that lets you know.

O.

Omnichannel marketing: An approach to marketing that creates an integrated experience for audiences no matter what device they're using or which platform they use to interact with a brand.

Organic reach: The number of unique users who view your content without paid promotion. People find social content organically through their news feeds—either from companies whose pages they've liked themselves, or shared by friends or connections.

P.

Pay per click (PPC): Also known as cost per click (CPC), a type of advertising where an organization pays each time a user clicks on an advertisement. The costs incurred during a PPC campaign vary based on the competitiveness of the keyword phrase an organization is targeting with its ads.

Permalink: The URL of an individual piece of content. Permalinks allow you to directly reference a specific piece of content instead of searching for it in the feed or timeline where you found it. You can quickly find an item's permalink by clicking on its timestamp.

Phishing: An attempt to fraudulently acquire sensitive information such as usernames, passwords, or credit card information through authentic-looking electronic communication, usually email. Also, a method of spreading electronic viruses by exploiting security weaknesses.

Q.

Quora: A Q&A website where anyone can ask their questions or answer other users' questions. For businesses, Quora can be a fantastic way to establish thought leadership or authority on a certain topic, or interact with users likely to be interested in their products or services.

R.

Reach: A data metric that determines the maximum potential audience for any given message. It is not a guarantee that the entire audience will see your social media post.

Reach is determined by a fairly complex calculation that includes number of followers, shares, and impressions, as well as net follower increase over time.

Real-time marketing: The practice of connecting with an online community around current events, trends, and customer feedback — often to a fault. If hopping on a hashtag bandwagon or personalizing a meme to your business isn't on the brand (ahem, dental offices still doing the Harlem Shake), it could fall flat with followers.

Recommendation: A term used to describe a written note from another LinkedIn member that aims to reinforce the user's professional credibility or expertise

Retargeting: An online advertising technique that aims to re-engage website visitors who left a site without converting. (If you've ever been followed around on the Internet by that pair of shoes you were drooling over during lunch, you've been retargeted.) Retargeting starts with a small tracking tag embedded in your website's code. Once visitors come to your website, you can then target them as they visit other websites, including search engines, social media sites, news outlets, and blogs.

The rationale is that these visitors are your best chance to make a sale, so instead of advertising to strangers, you spend your budget on prospects who have already visited your website.

Reply: A response to someone's tweet. Unlike direct messages, replies are public.

Response rate: An engagement metric used to assess how much you are interacting with your social audience. To calculate your response rate, take the number of mentions that you have replied to in a given time period, and divide it by the total number of mentions you have received (excluding retweets).

Response volume: The total number of outbound messages that an organization, team, or specific social media account delivers in response to customer service issues within a given time.

Return on investment (ROI): It measures the gain or loss generated on an investment relative to the amount of money invested. ROI is usually expressed as a percentage and is typically used for personal financial decisions, to compare a company's profitability or to compare the efficiency of different investments.

Return on relationship (ROR): A measurement of the value gained by a person or business from developing a relationship. Measuring ROR isn't easy — it involves not only analyzing connection growth but also understanding the impact your customers' voices have on your brand and reputation. This includes sentiment analysis, as well as engagement metrics for your content, like organic sharing rates.

RSS: A format for syndicating web content (short for Rich Site Summary or Simple Syndication, depending on who you ask; neither is an official acronym). RSS feeds are created in a standard XML format that makes them compatible with a variety of readers and aggregators.

Content creators use RSS feeds to broadcast content (or content summaries) to audiences. Readers can subscribe to RSS feeds without providing personal information, and then automatically receive updates through a newsreader or aggregator. RIP Google Reader.

S.

Scheduling: Planning social media updates and content ahead of time, using a social relationship platform (SRP), or another publishing tool. Scheduling saves social professionals time in their daily workflows by allowing them to draft several messages at once, often as part of a publishing approval process. It also enables them to reach audiences in different time zones and organize extended marketing campaigns.

SEO: The practice of increasing the "organic" visibility of a web page in a search engine, such as Google. Although businesses can pay to promote their websites on search engine results pages (Search Engine Marketing or SEM), SEO refers to "free" tactics that enhance the search ranking of a page.

Share of voice: A measure of how many social media mentions a particular brand is receiving about its competition. Usually measured as a percentage of total mentions within an industry or among a defined group of competitors.

Shortlink: URL shortening is a technique on the World Wide Web in which a Uniform Resource Locator (URL) may be made substantially shorter and still direct to the required page. This is achieved by using a redirect that links to the web page that has a long URL.

SlideShare: A popular social platform for sharing presentations and other business-oriented content. SlideShare makes it easy to embed content on websites and share it with other social networks, such as Facebook, Twitter, and LinkedIn (which has owned the platform since 2012).

Social commerce: An area of digital commerce where the buying process is assisted by social media and online networks.

Social listening: The process of finding and assessing what is being said about a company, topic, brand, or person on social media channels.

Social relationship platform: Secure, scalable technologies that allow businesses to manage social media communications of any kind across departments and devices. Think of a social relationship platform as a digital command and control: These tools put everything you need for social media in one place, making it easier to manage. Social relationship platforms are used for monitoring, posting, and tracking social media, and help manage everything from customer service to lead generation. Hootsuite is a social relationship platform.

Social proof: Social proof refers to a psychological phenomenon in which people seek direction from those around them to determine how they are supposed to act or think in a given situation. In social media, social proof can be identified by the number of interactions a piece of content receives or the number of followers you have. The thought is that if others are sharing something or following someone, it must be good.

Social selling: The use of social media by sales professionals to increase productivity and generate revenue. Sellers can effectively leverage social media to enhance their reputations, expand their interpersonal networks, and attract new prospects. They can also identify buyers by listening and engaging in the online spaces where potential customers are conducting research and asking for advice.

StumbleUpon: StumbleUpon is a free web browser extension that acts as an intelligent browsing tool for discovering and sharing web sites.

Spam: Unnecessary and repetitive content that clogs up in boxes and clutters social media feeds. In other words, the bane of your existence.

Sponsored posts: Content on a social media site that has been paid for by a brand or organization. Every social media platform has its form of sponsored content; brands can leverage sponsored content to get visibility with a larger audience that might be interested in their messages, products, or services.

T.

Tag: A keyword added to a social media post with the original purpose of categorizing related content. You can also tag someone in a post or photo, which creates a link to their social media profile and associates them with the content. Many services also offer the option to remove unwanted tags from your profile.

Terms of service: The rules individuals must follow to use a product or service. Every social platform has a detailed set of terms of service (ToS for short) that you agree to when creating a profile; if at any point you violate those terms, you can be banned from the service or have your account deleted. Users should take care to understand the agreements they sign when joining a social media site, including the terms of service and privacy policy; these documents are legally binding contracts.

Thread: A string of messages that make up a conversation. Threads begin with an initial message and then continue as a series of replies or comments.

Threads are essential to most forms of online communication, including social media and email.

Without them, it's extremely difficult to keep track of ongoing conversations.

Timestamp: The date and time that a message is posted to a social network, usually visible near the post's title or corresponding username. Clicking on a timestamp will usually bring you to the content's permalink.

Trend, trending: A topic or hashtag that is popular on social media at a given moment. Trends are highlighted by social networks such as Twitter and GAB encourages discussion and engagement among their users. The "trending" concept was first popularized by many social media platforms.

Triage: The process of prioritizing, assigning, and responding to inbound social media messages. The term is borrowed from emergency medicine, where it is crucial to assess the relative urgency of every case to prioritize care.

In a social media triage process, incoming messages are filtered, evaluated for urgency, assigned to the necessary parties, and, if necessary, escalated so that the organization can provide the appropriate response (either online, offline, or both).

Troll: A social media user who makes a deliberately offensive or annoying posting with the sole aim of provoking other users.

Tumblr: A microblogging platform that allows users to post text, images, video, audio, links, and quotes to their blog. Users can also follow other blogs and repost other users' content to their blog.

U.

URL: Short for Uniform Resource Locator, the location of a website page, or other resources on the Internet.

URL shortener: A tool that condenses a URL into a shorter (and more social media-friendly) format. Users who click on a short link are redirected to the original web address. URL shorteners, such as Bitly or ow.ly, can also provide link tracking capabilities, which allow businesses to measure click-throughs from social media and attribute website conversions to individual social messages.

User-generated content: Media that has been created and published online by the users of a social or collaboration platform, typically for non-commercial purposes. User-generated content is one of the defining characteristics of social media.

Many companies have enthusiastically embraced and encouraged user-generated content as a means of increasing brand awareness and customer loyalty. User-generated campaigns (such as Instagram contests) allow businesses to tap into the creative energies of their customers and use the contributions to fuel ongoing marketing tactics.

V.

Vanity URL: A web address that is branded for marketing purposes. Vanity URLs are customized to replace common URL shortener formats with something more closely related to an organization's branding. For example, instead of ow.ly or bit.ly, Time Inc.'s vanity URL is ti.me. The New York Times uses nyti.ms.

Verified: An account whose owner has proven their identity with the social media platform provider. This is usually reserved for brands, journalists, and other public figures as a way of preventing fraud and protecting the integrity of the person or organization behind the account.

Views: In reference to Snapchat, these are users who have looked at your Snap Story. To see who has viewed their story, users simply need to click the eye symbol next to their Story.

Viral: A term used to describe an instance in which a piece of content - YouTube video, blog article, photo, etc. - achieves noteworthy awareness. Viral distribution relies heavily on word of mouth and the frequent sharing of one particular piece of content all over the Internet.

Vlogger: Someone who creates and broadcasts video blogs.

W.

Webinar: A portmanteau of the word's "website" and "seminar," a digital broadcast of a presentation intended to educate or inform. Webinars allow users to see or hear a presentation from their computer or other devices and often interact directly with the presenter or fellow attendees through chat or video.

Rumble: Can be used as a noun to describe the website on which users upload, store, and share videos, or as a verb to describe the practice of consuming/creating content from/for the website

References

Buffa, J. (2013, February 13). *Cisco.* Retrieved from https://blogs.cisco.com/socialmedia/youtube-and-the-customer-journey?dtid=osscdc000283

Collier, A. (2019). *Contant Contact* . Retrieved from https://blogs.constantcontact.com/why-social-media-marketing/#

Corona, B. (2018, Feburary). Retrieved from https://www.bluecorona.com/blog/local-seo-nap-consistency-guide

Heing, I. (2018, June). *The State of Tech.* Retrieved from https://themanifest.com/social-media/7-reasons-consider-paid-social-media-advertising

Hootsuite . (n.d.). Retrieved from https://hootsuite.com/pinterest

Hubspot. (n.d.). Retrieved from https://www.hubspot.com/youtube-marketing

MacDonald, J. (2017, May). *Business 2 Community* . Retrieved from https://www.business2community.com/social-media/importance-hashtags-know-use-01837644

Pinkham, R. (2019). *Constant Contact* . Retrieved from https://blogs.constantcontact.com/what-is-linkedin/

readyartwork. (n.d.). Retrieved from https://www.readyartwork.com/business-video-marketing-strategy/

Readyartwork . (n.d.). Retrieved from https://www.readyartwork.com/business-video-marketing-strategy/

Shaw, B. (2019). *SEO Expert* . Retrieved from https://seoexpertbrad.com/dominate-local-seo-marketing/

Small Business . (n.d.). Retrieved from https://www.sba.gov/sites/default/files/March_April_2016_FINAL_508_compliant.pdf

Small Business Administration . (n.d.). Retrieved from https://www.sba.gov/

US Small Business Administration. (n.d.). Retrieved from https://www.sba.gov/sites/default/files/FAQ_March_2014_0.pdf
"glorified blog".

Author Bio

Lizzy McNett (pen name Anna Elizabeth Judd) is the founder and CEO of Writer's Publishing House and Ghost Writer Media. With more than eighteen years of experience, she has helped hundreds of authors bring their books to life and achieve bestselling status across multiple genres.

She holds a BA in Fine Arts with a minor in Equine Science and studied under renowned Western artist Robert "Shoofly" Shufelt at the Scottsdale Art Institute. Her deep background in horse training inspired several of her own novels, while her passion for storytelling led her to become a highly sought-after ghostwriter of bestselling books.

A proud America First entrepreneur, Lizzy founded Writer's Publishing House on the belief that every client deserves exceptional service and real success. She is known for her hands-on approach and genuine commitment to helping authors turn their passion into profit.

When she's not writing or guiding clients through the publishing process, Lizzy enjoys hiking, biking, and

spending time outdoors. Although she no longer trains horses professionally, their spirit remains a lasting part of her soul and her stories.
She lives by the simple philosophy: "Everyone should profit from their passion."

If you want to know more about publishing a book, please visit her website at https://writerspublishinghouse.com where you can contact her about starting your book project today.

Anna's Books: annaelizabethjudd.com

- IAuthor – Social Media Marketing Guide
- The Broken Angel
- The Handbook of Horsemanship
- The Broncobusters
- The Hourglass of el Diablo
- Marshal Spur and the Outlaw
- The Boy Who Couldn't Talk
- Spur Up! – Music Album
- Hey, Hay Learn Your ABC's
- Learn Your ABCs with Haystack
- A Distant Calling
- Skimmer's Adventure

www.ingramcontent.com/pod-product-compliance
Lightning Source LLC
LaVergne TN
LVHW051048220926
848485LV00001BA/45